THE
TRUTH
ABOUT
SECRETS

A MEMOIR-IN-VERSE

By Hazel Kight Witham

THE TRUTH ABOUT SECRETS

A Memoir-in-Verse

ISBN: 9781790998081

Published in the United States by
~~Strikethrough~~ Press
Los Angeles, California

First printing edition 2024.

Cover Art: Hazel Kight Witham
Cover Design: Eileen Dikdan Pottinger

For my Mamas, my Maps

and my Boys, my Buoys

A NOTE FROM YOUR AUTHOR:

This is a true story.

Some names have been changed
to protect the innocent.

Some names have been changed
to give the bullies and the betrayers

a break.

May we all have mercy
on our middle school selves.

blessing the boats
By Lucille Clifton

(at St. Mary's)

may the tide
that is entering even now
the lip of our understanding
carry you out
beyond the face of fear
may you kiss
the wind then turn from it
certain that it will
love your back   may you
open your eyes to water
water waving forever
and may you in your innocence
sail through this to that

Prologue: Pride Before the Fall

It was a gray June morning, but West Hollywood was bursting with rainbows everywhere we looked.

Luminous men aboard flowered floats, short shorts and high-top boots, chaps and flannel muscle tanks, unbuttoned to bare bright beating hearts to wide open air.

Women saddled atop motorcycles, bandanna-ed hair, leather vests and leather pants, motorcycle boots I fell in love with, some stacked two to a bike, arms around waists, calling themselves by names they'd embraced.

Others who somewhere were called Two-Spirit: both male and female, yet something beyond both. Sequins and gold lamé and long flowing wigs, sculpted legs and narrow hips, high heels and fishnets, shining like stars on Earth.

The power of that Milky Way flashing by, the cheering, whooping, whirling wildness of celebrating something that was supposed to be hushed and secret, quiet and closeted.

It was 1985, and I was ten, toeing the boundary-line between childhood and adolescence. My blond hair feathered in new breeze, my thin frame shimmered in glittered unicorn shirt and turquoise shorts, small chest puffed with some new thing I'd never known.

That morning marked 16 years since the Stonewall Uprising of June 1969, the revolt against police brutality and societal bigotry, though ten-year-old me knew nothing of that yet. How a protest could pave the way for a parade was something that would take a long time to understand. The chants around us, filling our lungs in grand chorus: *"Hey hey, ho ho, homophobia's got to go!" "Out of the closets, Into the streets!"*

This was the closest I'd ever been to celebrity, so many stars that never saw the shine of screen. To see this rainbow community celebrated on the streets, under such wide skies was a revelation.

How we all loved each other in that public space: cheering, whooping, whirling and wild on the sidelines and streets, smiles like starshine, so bright that the secrets in our mouths were swept out and up and away, for one glorious day.

PART ONE:

THE DAY EVERYTHING CHANGED

THE BOTTOM DROPS OUT
~February, 1987: Sixth Grade

The day is hummingbirds and hope
steady pulse of *Will he ask me? Will he ask me? Will he ask me?*

In the locker room
I lean into the mirror with other sixth-graders
drag blue eyeshadow across lids
arrange the features of the girl I see
into arched eyebrows, flirty pout, *Seventeen* magazine cute
try to pretend she's me.

I wait for the bell
peg and re-peg my jeans so they tightbite my ankles
over my scuffed Keds, wondering: *if-how-when-will he ask me?*
practicing in my head how I will say *Yes:*
pause, pursed lips, bright eyes, blink blink
like those gorgeous actresses on the big screen.

Then a girl I barely know walks toward me
one of Leyla the Beautiful's many friends.

She is flanked by two others
looks at me from

eyes
to
toes
toes
to
eyes

lips curling up at the edges
a little jerk of her head, hand on hip
that war pose girls assume
so many times a day, readying for battle.
Says, with a mean-smug smile in her voice:

"CAN I ASK YOU SOMETHING?"

The World Slows its Spin

I notice in the moments before:

gum-spattered constellations of
dark gray ick
dotting the concrete

the wall next to the gym
slashed in sun

us in shadow

this girl's face
illuminated:

something delicious
melting on her tongue

and some tiny

FRANTIC

part of me
knows what is coming
as the words unfold
from her sour mouth:

"Is it true? About your mom?"

Ice-cold terror tightening once-warm veins.

Elephant stampede across humming-winged heart.

The day has finally come.

THE LIST OF FEARS ABOUT MIDDLE SCHOOL

That people would make fun of
>> my awful glasses
>> my outfits
>> my hair
>> my flat chest
>> my pale skin, zit-freckled

That I would forget
>> my locker combination
>> my way to class
>> how to "Just Say No"
>> deodorant

That I would face
>> changing in front of people in the locker room
>> the fact that I closed my eyes when playing catch
>> an onslaught of bullies and I would *have* to fight them

That I would realize
>> my friends from elementary
>> weren't cool enough for middle school
>> and I would have to pretend I didn't know them

Worse: That *I* wasn't cool enough
>> and they would pretend they didn't know *me*

That I would have nothing interesting to say
That No Boy Would Ever Like Me

And: My Secret

So Secret I didn't even put it on the list.

And It was, BY FAR

the Most Terrifying Thing of All.

In Between the Asking and the Answering

You learn something about yourself
in moments like these.

Who are you when the truth comes calling?

Do you own it
or abandon it?

Do you stand
or do you run?

The sun slanted across that concrete wall
like the truth cutting through six years of shadow.

The glare of her stare
the words that were there

between us:

Is it true about your mom? Is it true about your mom?
IsItTrueAboutYour Mom? Is. It. True?

Those words swallowed everything, so fast
I barely registered the moment that had vanished:

all that hope of being chosen
the sweet question from a boy
replaced by the interrogation of a girl.

Her eyes piercing mine
predator locked to prey
asking really:

Who are you?
The answer:

                                              I was a coward.

The Origin of Secrets

Mom was a tomboy from always—happier running barefoot and bare-chested in jean cutoffs through the sighing heat of Texas summers. Her best friends were boys, she hated indoor play, hated dolls, hated skirts.

Secrets are bottled in our blood, passed down from our parents before we even know what an inheritance is. Mine were born with my mom in that small town of Orange, Texas.

See, my mom kept *her mom* a secret, the way she stayed in bed, so often sad, quiet, sleeping. How she was sent away sometimes when the dark got too dark. My mom didn't talk about her mom to her friends. And maybe they didn't ask.

I know my mom's mom had secrets too, because my mom told me little bits of grandma's life—a sadness she carried everywhere except on those many days it soured inside her and she didn't leave the bed. The bottle of "Red Medicine" on the bedside table that offered escape.

My mom's daddy drank too, but was also the provider, and probably the person my mom loved most.

My mom: a girl who dreaded starting school because it meant dresses instead of denim, classrooms and desks where she had to behave, sit nicely, be a proper young lady.

All the while another secret was brewing in that small-town girl, though it would be many years and many miles before she figured it out. Even longer before I learned what it meant.

THE EIGHTIES: A PRIMER

There's a lot going on.

The Space Shuttle Challenger explodes.
Seven lives lost
73 seconds after lift-off.
Christa McAuliffe, the first teacher heading to space
never returns home.

The War on Drugs and Just Say No.
Something called Crack, a demon drug.

The Iran-Contras affair and people in power lying.
The Soviet Union opening and the Berlin Wall falling.

Our President, the actor, Ronald Reagan
who likes jelly beans and fights Cold Wars.

AIDS, the "Gay" disease
that isn't just affecting gay people.

President Reagan has not even said the word: *AIDS*
like if he does it might become real
or he might catch it
or the "Religious Right" who helped boost him into office
might get offended.

The silence that surrounds
Gayness
and AIDS

and families that are not
one-mom-one-dad traditional

is

DEAFENING.

A Note from Your Author:

What I wish I'd known:

That it is important to question things

that you see

or don't see

on the news.

The news is not the whole story.

THE EIGHTIES: A PERSONAL PRIMER

But for me the Eighties is this:

Michael Jackson's *Thriller* and "Billie Jean"
the cringy wriggle of that word: *lover*.

"We Are The World," teaching us about famine and Egypt
Culture Club, Boy George: the ripe colors of his dreams.

Madonna's *True Blue* that Samantha and I
danced to and sang to non-stop:
the simplicity of islands and true blue love
between a boy and a girl.

Stand By Me, and delicious River Phoenix, growing up in 1959
the title song, "Stand By Me:"
night and moon and eternal loyalty
"Everyday" and the sweet rollercoaster of innocent love.

MTV, which I don't have, teaching everyone who does
what's cool, how to dance, and what music to listen to.

Judy Blume's *Are You There God? It's Me, Margaret*:
puberty and periods and religion.

Cynthia Voight's *Izzy, Willy-Nilly*:
a girl who loses her leg to a drunk driver.

The Trixie Belden series makes solving mysteries
an exciting teen career option.

The Black Stallion series feeds my horse-crazed heart.

Guess jeans with the red triangle patch on the back pocket that
broadcasts cool.
Esprit coordinating outfits that show
if your parents have money.

(I don't own any Esprit.)
Pegged jeans rolled to snug-hug calves
but which always come loose.
Tee-shirts with rolled sleeves
that always come unrolled.

Girls are always in a state of pegging or rolling
or just finishing pegging or rolling
or noticing someone else's need for pegging or rolling.

Cool boys flowing SoCal chill:
Jimmy'z shorts, OP surf shirts, Vans.
Like they are skaters and surfers
not kids hanging on bikes and lawns.

Some kids wear Ray Bans, even to school.
Feathered hair is everywhere.
Wet 'n' Wild nail polish chips moments after application.
Jelly shoes and jelly bracelets, jean jackets and slouch socks.

There is always the hustle:
trying to keep up with the newest look
the coolest song, the best of everything.

Sometimes all I can manage when I come home
after a long day of attempting middle school cool

is burying myself
in a book

where everything is clear
right there on the page

and I can read and reread
to better understand.

A Note from Your Author:

Remember what we didn't have back in the late eighties:
Mainstream LGBTQIA+ Representation.

No *Ellen*, no *Will and Grace*, no *RuPaul's Drag Race*
No *Queer Eye*, no *Modern Family*, No, Nope, None.

Sure, Out and Proud might parade the streets of
West Hollywood
but all Hollywood put on TV
was simpering lisps and floppy wrists
lazy jokes about sashaying side characters.

Oh—and also? Get this:

No Smartphones. No Internet.

No Apps that can make Rumor-Share/Smack-Talk/Photo-Fails
Go VIRAL.

BRONJA

My "sister" Bronja (*Bron-ya*) is an exchange student from Germany: short, dark hair, cute bright eyes, 18-years-old, an accent that makes you pay attention. She teaches me staccato German curse words.

Bronja is my mom's student at a nearby high school. Funny, how my mom, hater of school, went on to create a career as a teacher, spend her whole working life in a classroom.

Bronja started in a difficult family placement and became close to my mom over the first half of the school year. I remember the conversation that led her to our door, back when we had a door, before the house was overhauled and gutted and the remodeling began, last month, late January. The question:

"How would you like to have a sister?"

A new sun dawning across a bright blue world.

It would be temporary, of course, and she wouldn't be at my school, but I could call her my sister, feel for the first time what siblinghood might be like~ sharing a family, sharing a room, sharing clothes, someone around my age I could pour my heart out to.

"Yes, yes! When can I meet her?"

She moved in three days before demolition began. We had two nights sharing my double bed talking late, swapping stories, sharing secrets. But on the third day, rains came and caved in the compromised roof while we were at school. A hole above the closet, a dampness in the room, a view of overcast sky where there had never been one. My childhood room gaping, bare bones exposed to the world. So much to clean up.

We moved into the trailer that was to be our temporary home for the bulk of the remodel, shoved our dressers and boxes into the garage, ferried changes of clothes back and forth every few days.

It wasn't long before the shine wore off and I started to feel the choke of living bare bones exposed, so near someone else~ the scooting past her, the constant *"Excuse me's"* the waiting for the teeny-tiny bathroom, the having someone see me in the morning before I am ready to be seen~that closet-less space, where I changed in the bathroom and stashed my clothes in corners.

Soon all those bright blue hopes of sisterhood~sharing a family, sharing a room, sharing clothes, sharing secrets~start to cloud over.

The Day, from Dawn: Before School

I wake up to Bronja's
grumpy rustling in the bunk below me.

I remember what today is, the thrum of
—*Will he ask me? Will he*—
beating as I *BASH* my head against the
stupid low ceiling of the trailer.

I hate living in a trailer.
Even if it's temporary.

I swivel my legs over the edge
roll to my belly, dangle my toes, shove off
quick tap off her leg
Owwmmm!!
—*Sorry, Bronja!*—
and hit the floor.

I walk the four linoleum steps to the bathroom
slide in, click the door closed, and pivot to sit.
I can lean and touch the crinkled floral plastic paneling
in front of me
with my forehead if I want to.

I wash my hands in the cereal bowl sink
and when I look in the mirror
I see pink skin freckled with baby zits
unobtrusive but everywhere
one of the many visible curses of puberty.

Blue eyes are my only hope at Pretty.
How do I get people to not see my skin and only my eyes?

I long for the makeup I play with at Samantha's house
still forbidden to me in sixth grade.

I count the long months until seventh~
March, April, May, June, and then

"Maybe."

"We'll see."

"I have to think about it."

"I'll talk to Sharon."

My mom doesn't get it.
I *need* makeup, *especially* today.

PRIMPING FOR JACK

It is all about the hair
since it can't be about the makeup.

Last night I thought of Jack as I pincurled my hair
sitting on the stupid hard foam trailer couch
that turns into a bed for Bronja at night.
How our phone calls are shivery
and I am edge-of-my-seat nervous
looking for how to get a laugh
and the triumph of confirmation when I do.

Separate a section, twist, twist, twist, *Jack*
swirl against the scalp, *Jack*
bobby pin from mouth, *Jack*
stab through the coil, *Jack*
hold breath hope it holds, *Jack*
repeat, *Jack*.

How tall guy with cool eyes will be passport to Pretty
to special, to cool, to *KISS*.

Repeat repeat repeat repeat
Jack Jack Jack Jack
as arms aloft grow achy and fingers fumble.

Beauty has a price, and it's bought with time.

I went to bed on my bunk with
my 18-inch headroom, my head on the pillow, *Jack*
all 18-pinch-poke pincurled-prickles, *Jack*
and wondered where it would happen:

behind the cafeteria?
beside my locker?
leaning against chainlink?

If it will happen,
WHEN it happens.

Got to think positive.
Remembering the whispers: *I heard it's between you and Leyla.*

Leyla.
Leyla the Beautiful.
Leyla of dark eyes dark hair dark lashes
skin olive and flawless

who never needs makeup
but is probably allowed it anyway.

THE MAKEUP GAME

The girls' bathroom turns beauty parlor
on middle school mornings
when girls who can't leave the house with makeup

~but who aren't bothered by defying their parents~

cluster at the mirrors early
when the light is aluminum
and the metallic stare of the glass is more forgiving
than the looks on other kids' faces.

They lean in, mouths in silent O's
drawing the eyes that they see on screens and magazines.
Shimmery blue eyeliner, smudgy kohl black.

They hold their palettes of colors:
quartets of frosted blues and purples and greens and browns
dab with tiny wands.

Little magicians.
They become brighter, prettier versions of themselves.
They make their faces into magnets to draw admiring eyes.

Sometimes they are making magic with each other:
You would look soooo cute with a little eyeliner
a bit of powder, here, let me curl your lashes

Peacock primping, feathering each other's possibility.

I could do it too.
I could pack makeup in one of my backpack pockets.
I could rush to the bathroom first thing.
I could put Samantha's makeup practice into play
make myself someone I can stand to see.

Who I can stand Jack to see.

But I don't want to have to remember
to take the makeup off before the end of the day.

I don't like lying. I do it enough already:

I like your outfit.

He's really nice.

This is my mom's friend, Sharon.

BUT THIS MORNING

I slide into my not-Guess jeans
and my billowing pink button-up yes-Guess shirt.
Even though pink and I have never gotten along~
my face is pink enough,
and I've always felt more tomboy than girly-girl~
but the shirt was on sale
and I traded color for brand name.

I peg the bottoms of my jeans to bite my ankles
pull white slouch socks on with white Keds.
Try to dismiss the thought that
I'm some skewed version of
Miss Middle School America in red white and blue.

Pull out all the bobby pins, spray the springy coils
before loosening them with fingers and fluffing my blond hair
~wishing it could look something like
beautiful eighth grader Jamie Allay's
one of the girls I secretly wish I could be~
hoping that Jack asks me before nutrition break
when the curls will start to collapse.

And then: after Mom collects the bowls from breakfast
leaves the trailer to go get her purse

Shhh…
I slide lipgloss and eyeshadow into my backpack.

This morning I might be one of *those* girls
primping at the mirror.

Sometimes you have to break the rules.
Sometimes secrets are sweet.

Especially if you don't
have to cover them with lies.

A Note from your Author:

Yep, four chapters on primping.
School hasn't even started yet.

What I wish I'd known:
All the time spent in painful pin-curling
never added up to thick hair, and never fooled anyone.

Makeup was a mask, and I looked fine without it.
No one cared: they were too worried about themselves.

I was trying way too hard to distance myself from my family
and I wish I could have just embraced them
instead of performing the game of boy-crazy
so intently that no one would ever assume otherwise.

Have you noticed?
I can't even tell *YOU* my secret…

SCHOOL, EARLY MORNING

Before school can be a treacherous time
when your friends might not have come yet
and you are forced to find temporary friends
who will answer your constant need for company.

A few familiar forms come into my blurry view:

There's the sweet girl, Abby
who is so tall and gangly and gentle
she reminds me of a giraffe.

There's my former crush
huge-hearted, sky-high kind guy.
I used to look forward to his hugs every day.
He's with some of his friends
so that would be weird.

There's the girl with the unfortunate hairstyle
who has a scent of desperation
I am afraid might rub off.

There's Surly Girl, popular with boys, savage with girls
both the ones in her crew and those outside it.
Surly Girl, who I try to both steer clear of
and be liked by.

There's Iris,
Short cute dynamic funny pretty
always with the perfectly paired brand name outfits.

I don't know why we don't like each other
but I secretly wish we did.

I pick Abby and go over and say hello.
Then she wants to go say hi to *Iris*.

                                        Great.

WAITING

Abby and I walk over to Iris's locker
where she's wrestling her books
into the slim space like
it's a comedy routine she's perfected.

Her social studies book spills out
and catches her binder on the way down
and in an avalanche of ridiculous
her papers are everywhere
and she's laughing like she's embarrassed
but also so comfortable laughing at herself
it makes everyone else laugh too
and I'm picking up English notes and math homework
before I remember we don't like each other.

Something about her makes me so irritated:
her natural beauty and permission to wear makeup
her shortness, which makes all boys fair game
her curviness, which I would give anything for
her sense of humor, which is infectious to anyone nearby
her Esprit and Guess ensembles
that are so frustratingly perfect on her.

I guess it's a lot of things.
But mainly just one:
she doesn't seem to like me at all.

Abby and I hand her back her things
and when Iris's hands are free
she gives Abby a good-morning hug

and I just stand there.

See Ya

I see a flash of red across the walkway
and wave to Abby
and hope Iris notices
I've shunned her right back
even if I did help her pick up her stuff.

I head over to where Samantha
~my oldest friend, the closest I've got to a sister
red-headed, freckles, familiar and safe~
hangs with one of her friends from elementary.

I usually feel like the
not-wanted almost-sister
but I'll take third wheel
over invisible any day.

The thing is, even with sisterish Sam
I can't talk about the hummingbirds in my chest today
my whole-body hoping that Jack will ask me
because I don't think Samantha
will be too excited that I might be going with someone
by the end of the day
and she is not.

I don't want to throw a net
over my humming hopes
by sharing with people who may not want
to know.

I chew my cheek while we chat
about the homework for Ms. Feuerstein
and scan the gathering groups
for

Jack.

JACK ANDERSON

In case I haven't mentioned
my crush is a blond-haired, blue-eyed boy named Jack.

He has a deep voice, even at 11
and he is taller than me by a good couple inches
always my first requirement for a crush.
I am one of the taller girls
cursed with having to wait for boys to catch up.

Nothing spoils flirting like looking down at a guy.
Girls aren't supposed to be bigger than boys.

We're supposed to look up at them, bat our eyes
be cute and petite and ready to be enfolded in a hug.
All the movies and magazines and shows tell us so.

Jack's pale blond hair swoops across his forehead
so that sometimes it hides one eye.
One perfect blue eye.

He wears a mild smirk most of the time
one of those laid back
bordering on too-cool-for-school boys
though he is smart enough to answer questions in class
stumping teachers who think they've busted him.

We talk on the phone when I can steal trailer time alone and
I have bubbles inside me, butterflies, hummingbirds.
I feel like I am sitting on the edgedy-edge
of the hard foam couch
like if I laugh too hard I might fall off.

I have to balance along the risky ridge of conversation
trying not to say anything too dumb
but also trying not to be so safe I'm boring.

In class I steal looks at him
hoping he'll look back.
When he gives me that one-eyed smirk
I feel a giggle in my whole body.

I wonder what it would be like to hold his hand
to get a hug that had more behind it than just friendship.

But then I start noticing who else he is noticing:

LEYLA THE BEAUTIFUL

HOMEROOM

I see Jack get to school just before
the tardy bell, walking with Sidekick.
Sidekick is a roly-poly kid
with glasses that slide down his sweaty nose.
I think he's half-Asian, but I'm not sure.

My friends—mostly white—don't really talk about race.

There's that hesitation before describing someone
as *Black*, or *African-American*, or *Latino*, or *half-this, half-that*
like the label itself might be offensive
like we aren't supposed
to acknowledge any difference
even though we all secretly do.

Just like I secretly did when
my crush was the
huge-hearted, sky-high kind guy
who was so nice, so funny
but somehow
he seemed off-limits, out-of-bounds
just because of his race:
part Black, part white, all cute.

And I wonder:
Why does it matter?
Who told me it does?
And why do I believe them?

Sidekick's got that too-eager scent about him
like he's always trying to impress
like he's never relaxed
never sure of himself.

A scent I secretly, horribly wonder if I too carry.

I want to amble over and say hello to Jack
flirt a little before school
but I don't want to do it in front of Sidekick.

And something tells me
IF today is the day
I probably should let Jack
miss me a little bit.

Let *him*
look for me.

GO-BETWEENS FOR GOING WITH

I hope Sidekick is not the go-between
for me and Jack.
Go-betweens are common
when someone asks you to
Go With Them.

A phrase I have never fully understood:
"Will you Go With Me?"
"Sure, but Go Where?"

I guess in middle school we keep it vague
because it's tough to ask someone on a date
to an actual location
when you are five years away
from having a driver's license.

I couldn't stand it if Sidekick
asked me out
for Jack.

That would not make me feel very fluttery.

A Note from your Author:

Yep, six chapters on navigating
before-school socializing.
This pivotal school day still hasn't started yet.

What I wish I'd known:
That every morning doesn't need to be a popularity contest.
That it's okay to like someone who's a different race than you.

That race is a system of identification humans created.
It is a social construct, which means it exists
because humans say it exists.
That I didn't need to let social constructs affect who I liked.

I'm pretty sure I would have been way happier
with that huge-hearted, sky-high kind guy.

He was so, so sweet.
And his hugs were delicious.

Period 1

Mr. Laddin's art class is a great way to ease into the day.
He is always grumpy~it's his shtick~
but I love it.

I love when he offers his reluctant compliments:
"Not too bad, Kight. You just might pass this one."
I always get an A.

Art has been a part of my life since I can remember:
Long hours trying to copy horses
out of books, onto the page
like if I could render them just so they might prance
off the newsprint, into my room.

Mr. Laddin has us working on the jigsaw now.
Cut a shape out of wood, paint it
incorporate the name of it in the shape.

I'm working on an umbrella
scalloped edges and a giant
J
for a handle, my secrets carved in wood.

I lose myself for a while in the sanding of the edges
the fine sweet sawdust powdering my hands
the smell so soothing
the back and forth of the sandpaper
a kind of meditation
that makes me forget for a few minutes
what a big deal today is.

Hopefully.

Art class gives me quiet space to think
while my hands are moving.
Today it's the scent of sawdust that takes me back.

The Island

I was six, just about to start first grade.

The really new New Girl.

My parents divorced when I was two
and I was living with my dad, full-time
in Washington State on an island
1200 miles from Los Angeles home
1200 miles that we drove in Dad's orange van, Naranja.

I spent the fall sharing a trailer with my dad
tucked under the eaves of a barn.

A trailer I tucked into while my dad
was fashioning the barn into a home, mostly by himself.
My first experience with the wonders of remodeling.
Pounding hammers the rhythm of my days
screeching saws and the smell of fresh cut wood.

I spent the fall tiptoeing around my father
on days when I could smell his bad mood
on days when people would visit the property
I did not know yet whether they were friend or foe.

There were so many eggshell times
when I had to tread so lightly my very breath felt too heavy.

But mostly I spent the fall falling in love with the land
the 100 acres of forests
fed by a pond and a lake
with high blond grass and barbed wire fences
blackberry bushes and dirt roads
that unspooled across low hills
bald eagles that carved cursive
into the big blue, often gray sky.

Land I walked with Suki
our German Shepherd-Malamute
with the white-fawn body, black saddle back
the closest I had to a sibling
the closest I had to a mom on that island.

I fell in love with the late nights
when we would eat dinner
and still be able to go outside afterward
walk in the violet breath of twilight
the dark settling in like our old dog circling the rug to sleep.

And the stars winked into the night and filled the sky
like no Los Angeles sky I'd ever seen.
My dad, a librarian cataloging the ancient lights:
Cassiopeia, Deneb, Castor and Pollux, Ursa Major
Orion the Hunter and Sirius, his loyal dog star.

My father's favorite: the hunter's dog
that followed his master into the galaxy's deep.

I loved that land.
The land made the New Girl-ness of school
and Mom-less-ness of Dad a bit more manageable.

Days of not knowing how I fit in with the Island kids
and afternoons, evenings, weekends
making that land into home
with a dog and a dad who was~
even with all those eggshell moments~
on pretty good behavior.

Land more beautiful than anything
I'd ever known in my Los Angeles home
where a Secret was being born in my absence.

THE TRUTH ABOUT SECRETS

That year on the island when I was six
I was already well-versed in my own secrets.

Small ones, like the gray plastic seal I stole
from Samantha when I was four, maybe five.
Samantha who I've known since diapers, since before knowing.

I remember taking the seal because I liked him
his seal nose balancing a ball on the tippy-tip.
I remember how small he was
how he fit so easily in my own small hand.
I remember balancing him on a shelf
looking at his gray seal body
trying to remember the sweet feeling I had before I took him.

Trying to forget that he belonged to my friend.
Trying to remember what he meant before he became a secret.

And Big ones, like Secrets from Dad.
Secrets about Mom.
That she doesn't love him anymore.
Which he should know, since they divorced when I was two
but for a while he didn't seem to really believe it was over.

There was always this unspoken sense
that he felt it was still his house
still his wife
and there was an ocean of things
I didn't understand about why they split up.

Even now I keep secret how she tenses up
whenever his barrel-chested bulk fills the air of our L.A. home.
I keep secret what I know in my bones:
that she is still scared of him.
I keep secret that some part of my body knows why
even if I can't remember it in my head.

Instead, I walk the tightrope between them
keeping things safe, keeping things secret
protecting what is delicate from his iron ox self.

And I keep secrets from Mom about Dad.
How sometimes he talks about her.
How he tells me to tell her he still loves her.
I did tell her that once, because he asked me to
because he didn't want it to be a secret
but I told her carefully so that she couldn't hear
like I could, the need in his voice.

The ache that I always wish I could heal.
The ache I can't take away no matter how much I try.

And I keep secrets from Dad about myself.
I don't tell him much of anything that is true.
That is real.
That is my heart.

Like how scared I am of him.
Like how I rarely want to go with him
for weekend visitations, how I feel the dread for days
then spend the days together tiptoeing through every moment
walking on eggshells.

I rarely talk about myself because he rarely asks me anything.
He is all talk talk talk talk talk talk talk.

Sometimes, lots of times, even now
early morning, art class, sawdust and memories
when I am almost six years past six
it seems I am tiny speck of nothing
with a galaxy of secrets swirling inside
so many quiet constellations no one
~not even I~

can name.

PASSING TIME

We store away our woodworking projects
and line up at the door to await the bell.
Laddin barks goodbye as the bell sounds
reminding me of my dad, gruff growls and bully bluster.

I head toward PE and see Emma and Vivienne.
Emma, beautiful, but completely unaware of her beauty:
flowing copper hair, down-to-earth laugh
a kinda-tomboy like me, a funny, good girl.

She's Best Friends with Vivienne, sweet, funny, shy.
When they are together: Vivienne & Emma, Emma & Vivienne
I feel like the third wheel. I feel like the third wheel a lot.

But sometimes Emma invites me over to her house
and we pull each other on a skateboard down a hill
one on bike, one on board, wind in our hair, speed in our veins
rumble in our toes from the grit-gravel-grip of the asphalt.

We pass notes in class and laugh about boys
but she's not boy-crazy like I am
so we don't really talk about them too much.
Though she knows that I'm waiting.

As we pass she gives me a little raised-eyebrow funny look
that Today might be The Day.

I see Jamie Allay
tall, pretty, sleepy-eyed eighth-grade Jamie Allay
way far away
too far for a quick hug.

The girl I wish was my sister
the girl I wish I could be
as I head across the walkway
into the locker room.

Period 2: Spark

Iris has her locker near mine in the locker room.
We change next to each other every day
and every day I am reminded that we
don't like each other.

We put our PE shirts on
over our tank tops and training bras
though she isn't really in training anymore.
Lucky.

We use the PE shirts over our heads for cover
slink our arms out of our regular shirts
and perform quick-change-magic
to hide our shy bodies.

Sideways glances and sussing-out as others get ready.
But never anything too obvious
for fear that someone might call you a *Lesbo*.
Which shouldn't matter but completely does.

I'm not sure which is worse:
the fear of being called *Lesbo*
OR
the shame of shunning *Lesbo*.

It is a fast scramble to make it out to the line
with the rest of the class.

Today is stretches and soccer and I try not to break a sweat
so that I'm not grimy-gross for the rest of the day, for Jack.

I'm so immersed in thinking of him
I don't notice the clusters of girls
gathering here and there.

The glances in my direction.

Floating

Cold shower and scratchy pink mini-towels
dressing and hiding
makeup and sneaking
primping and prepping

I step out of musty locker room
into cool concrete waiting area
stand in the lake
of the shade

think about
sky blue eyes meeting mine
swooshing blond waves
and a long thin boy.

I float in these thoughts
like I am in some
warm Caribbean sea
fine white sand below

mild blue waves rocking my back
golden sun painting my body
from above.

Anticipation a delicious dream.

THE TRUTH WILL OUT

They stand before me triumphant
war pose girl posse
smirk smile hand hip
sun-splashed truth
concrete lies
eyes to toes toes to eyes.

Their wolf grins and the question that comes
is not the one I have been prepping for.

The question that comes like the
G I A N T   B O U L D E R
in *Indiana Jones and the Raiders of the Lost Ark*
crashing down at the far end of the walkway so I see it:
massive, sky-giant, H U R T L I N G toward me
even before she says it:

"Is it True, About Your Mom?"

My mouth gapes
like a fish flung from warm sea
to cold unimaginable air.

"I—No—I mean, What did you hear?"

The bell rings.

THE B O U L D E R IS C R U S H I N G THE W O R L D

I don't wait for her answer.
I run.

In my footfalls and fear flight
the years smash over me:

my Secret history.

The Secret I Returned To

I can remember my mom's hug, that Christmas visit when I returned to L.A., midway through the Island year with dad, back when I was six. That hug, long and strong and home. How she crouched low to gather me in at my height. Her "Hey, Petunia Blossom!" and the warm sun of relief.

I felt like myself again. I could walk full-footed on solid ground. I could do no wrong, I was safe and valued and heard. I didn't have to keep any secrets, I didn't have to pretend. In that moment, I couldn't imagine returning to the Island.

This was my refuge, this was my home, this was my mom. There was Cindy, with her whip of a wagging tail, her woo-woo-woo bark, jumping on me, kissing my face.

This was my home. A real house with four walls that were already built, not part of a construction site, my art hanging above the fireplace, my room just the way I left it. A bed with matching sheets and blankets, my books on the shelves lining the wall, shelves dotted with picture frames and shiny things that glinted in the swallow of dark when I was trying to fall asleep.

Everything I ever knew, just as I had left it.

Except—

REFUGE

Run past the lockers

run to the bathroom

avoid all the eyes

avoid nutrition break

close myself in a stall.

Heave

heavy breaths

wracking silent *this-can't-be-happening* sobs

tears smear down my face, across my hands.

How do I contain this secret?

How do I keep the lie about my mom?

How do I keep denying Sharon?

How do I contain this Gargantuan Shame?

How do I say the words I'm not supposed to say?

The words I've been swallowing, all these years?

Sharon

I barely remember meeting her that December when I came home from the island for a visit. She was my mom's friend. She had an easy smile, clear blue eyes.

She was there Christmas morning when I was six, with presents.

I remember not knowing something. I remember wondering *why presents?* Why was she excited to meet me?

Someone else in our house, at home in our house, but not my mom or me.

There's a picture of her hugging me, with the Christmas tree behind us, but could we have been so comfortable so fast that she would put her arms around me?

When I left back in August it had been just me and my mom, Cindy the dog, and our home the only way I'd ever known it.

When I came home it had changed.

What had changed?

HIDDEN

I can hear girls at the sinks
as I lean against the stall's metal door.

Everything I ever knew
in upheaval:

my fear-heavy gut
my panic-wild mind.

They talk and laugh and toss
gossip chatter back and forth

through the mirrors where they
drag lip gloss across pursed pouts

and strain for
their place in Pretty.

Their talk
so casual.

Like the earth hasn't disappeared
beneath their feet

only mine.

None are falling

                    through the web of a lie

        they have spent

                            half their life assembling.

THE TALK

My mom and I sat on the side of her bed. My feet didn't reach the floor. I remember thinking it was so simple, the way she said it:

"Sometimes a man and a woman fall in love,
and sometimes a man and a man fall in love,
and sometimes a woman and a woman."

She didn't use the word *lesbian*.

For some reason, I don't know why, I remember thinking of old-fashioned nurses, maybe from the 50's, in white A-line dresses and those caps that were white starched crowns.

That was my image of a woman falling in love with a woman.

My mom had fallen in love with a woman.

Sharon. *Sharon.*

It didn't stay simple long.

A Note from your Author:

My mom was trying to describe the spectrum of sexuality,
and it made my kid brain stretch into new shapes.

She was telling me that there is more than just the
straight relationships that are represented EVERYWHERE.

Not only that, but that she was IN one of those
"other" kinds of relationships.

What I wish I'd known:
That along this spectrum of sexuality from straight to gay
there are lots of points in between.

That you might move around on the spectrum of attraction
over the course of your life.

That just because you don't see images of relationships
other than straight ones, doesn't mean that's all there is.

CALL FOR COURAGE

I don't know where I will find it
and my eyes are running out of options.

I'm pretty sure it's not here
in the scummy grout of the once-pink tile

of this girls' bathroom.
The lidless toilet gaping at me.

The little flocks of tissue paper
scattered across the floor.

The claw of realization
clamps around my heart:

I have to go out there.

I have to tell my friends
before they find out from someone else.

But how do I tell them?
How will they ever understand my family?

I take deep breaths
that do not relax me.

My secret world swims inside.
I try to find the peace that I once knew there.

I've never felt so terrified in my life.

WHAT WOULD SHARON DO?

After that eggshell year with my dad on the Island, I returned to Los Angeles, where home became three of us: Me, Mom, and Sharon. There were times I missed it just being me and my mom.

But Sharon brought something new into our life. A fun, a fearlessness, a love of music, a set of memories and stories different from my mom's. Tales of a Brooklyn childhood, a fighting family, an older brother, snow falling, long walks through the white to PS 206, stickball and kick-the-can.

But the most important thing she brought was calm. Ease.

Sharon didn't have anxiety like my mom. She didn't have worry. She didn't have fear. She was the most self-assured person I had met. No second-guessing, no indecision, no fretting about what was or what will be.

She had a 12-step Serenity Prayer card that shimmered from the dashboard of her blue Honda Civic:

"God, Grant Me the Serenity
to Accept the Things I Cannot Change
Courage to Change the Things I Can
and the Wisdom to Know the Difference."

Sharon's motto was "Why worry? It won't change anything anyway." "Don't borrow trouble" was another favorite, which meant the same thing— don't worry yourself into what might or might not be, just deal with what IS.

And "Feelings aren't facts," which hinted at some wise perspective I could hardly fathom. To me, feelings were everything.

Sharon brought a balance. Where my mom was always moving, doing, fretting, Sharon was an oasis of calm, stillness, peace. She was spacious, a woman of size and substance and strength and safety. I could go to her with my worries and she could shift my point of view and ease my mind. She was magic like that.

Especially when it came to dealing with my dad.

Like that one time after a weekend visitation with him, when he tried to pull some drop-off nonsense. She stood right up to him, fearlessly, in a way I'd never seen anyone do with my dad. I watched from the front window as she backed him up across the lawn and into his car, daring him to cross her, daring him to bully her or her family.

Which is to say, my mom and me. Sharon was magnificent like that.

How do I capture who she is, how *important* she is, in a few frantic words to friends who may not be friends for long?

What would Sharon say I should do?

HISTORY OF A SECRET

I stall behind the stall door
trying to remember the rules
for managing this secret.

When did my mom tell me
I might not want to tell people?

Was it before or after I told Eva?
Eva, the pretty girl with long wavy dark hair
3rd grade to my 2nd grade.
Eva who I wanted to like me.

How I forgot myself when she said that thing
about how two girls can't *like* like each other
and I blurted out:
"My mom has a girlfriend. She lives with us."

How she looked at me like I was from another planet
my words an unfathomable language.

Eva, daughter in a family of Jehovah's Witnesses
who didn't celebrate anything, not even her birthday
certainly not Pride.
Behind the stall door I can still feel her silence.
My sharing did not bring us closer.
She started to slip further away
like a ship disappearing over the horizon
and I learned the importance of keeping some things secret.

Was that when the shame was born?

I think about the four people I told
all of them because I wanted to
because I needed someone else to know, to tell me it was ok.

First: Samantha, who I'd known from always

who I told when we were wandering the church grounds
after Sunday School, before reception and cookies.
Samantha, whose mom was one of my mom's best friends
and who probably already knew
but who I had to tell to make it real.
Samantha, who seemed fine with it, who just shrugged
who didn't look at me like I was crazy or ruined somehow.

But with Samantha
I wasn't sure I could say that I wasn't sure how I felt
about my mom and Sharon
how I didn't like hiding things going on in my own home.
But at least it was out there, once, in the air between us.
At least I didn't have to lie to my oldest friend.

Second: Ruby, whose mom took me to their house
every day after school until my mom could pick me up.

Third: Natalie, who was friends with Ruby
and semi-friends with me.
I remember I told her in a rush of hoping
that she might like me more for confiding my secret.
I learned with her that secrets
could be a kind of currency you could trade:
if I trust you with this, maybe it will create a bond between us?

Fourth: Marie, 5th grade to my 4th
the brash, confident, funny girl who I loved hanging out with
because she had the courage to say anything she wanted.
She reminded me of Sharon:
confident, unconcerned about others' judgment.
Marie didn't seem to doubt herself
and didn't seem to judge me for my mom.

Four people I told on purpose.

Four people I told so I didn't have keep lying.

THE WAYS I LIED

I'd introduce her as "my mom's friend"
or "my mom's roommate"
or the worst:
"The woman who rents a room behind the garage."

Those sentences so self-conscious
I could hear the clunk and twang
of each lying syllable as it left my mouth.

Worse, maybe, was the acting.
Pretending I didn't love Sharon when
she happened to be in the same room with my friends.

Pretending I didn't have to listen to her like she was a parent.
Pretending I didn't have to ask her permission
to do things like I did with my mom.

No easy way to be the daughter of two women
who loved each other.

Lesbians.

No easy way to say it, ever.

Not the lie.

Not the truth.

None of it.

A Word about the L Word

I think about what I am going to go out there and say.

My mom is gay…please don't stop being my friend?
My mom is a lesbian, are you cool with that?

I have never liked the word *lesbian*.
I don't think Mom really uses it much either.
I think she said *gay* and that was easier on my ears.
Lesbian sounded like a word that needed to be whispered
like *Cancer*.
So concrete, so final, so serious, so possibly contagious.

Gay was cooler. It meant happy, joyous, buoyant.
Mom and Sharon were friends with some gay guys.
They owned who they were, they didn't seem to hide.
Unless, I guess, they did?

I can't actually name a single famous person
who is out and proud as gay or lesbian.
There are no role models that kids my age think are cool.

I only know the people my parents are friends with.
And I know the word gay in the wider world is an insult
but it's still somehow better than lesbian.

So I used the term gay.
For the first four people I told~Samantha, Ruby, Natalie, Marie~
I think I didn't even use that though.

"My mom's gay" was a little more label than I could handle in
elementary.

When I came clean, I think I just said
"My mom and Sharon are together."
or "Sharon is my mom's girlfriend."
I avoided those pesky labels as long as I could.

A Note from your Author:

What I wish I'd known:

The word "Gay" originally meant happy, flamboyant, carefree and then took on a sexual connotation in the 1600's, describing people unrestrained by societal norms and social constructs.

Eventually it began to be used within the gay community—people wanted a word less clinical-sounding than "homosexual."

The word "Lesbian" comes from people on the island of Lesbos where the poet Sappho lived, way back in 657BC-570BC well before other Ancient Queers like Sophocles and Plato. Sappho wrote and sang incredible lyric poetry praising women.

Back in the 80's, in the time of zero positive LGBTQIA+ representation, I could have used some ancient role models for alternative ways of loving.

In the Last Gasps

Before I head out into the
churning waters

with those
sharkfin flashes,

This:

A N G E R

Pounding fists against stupid salmon pink metal stall door

ANGER.

What did she THINK would happen?

WHY couldn't she just be NORMAL?

WHY couldn't she just be STRAIGHT?

A Note from your Author:

What I wish I'd known:

A bit more about the vivid array of experience and identity.

LGBTQIA+ =

Lesbian=Woman who is attracted to Women.

Gay=Person who is attracted to a Person
of one's own gender or sex.
And/Or
Genderqueer= A person who does not identify with
conventional gender distinctions and may identify with
neither, both, or a combination of male and female genders.

Bisexual=Person who is attracted to more than one gender.
There's also **Pansexual**=Person attracted to people
regardless of gender.

Transgender=Person who does not identify as the gender they were assigned at birth.
And/Or
Two-Spirit=Indigenous People's term for a third gender, with both Male and Female qualities.

Queer=A Rainbow person, anyone not on the strictly Straight spectrum
And/Or
Questioning=anyone wondering who they are or how they identify.

Intersex=Umbrella term that describes bodies that fall outside the strict male/female binary.

Asexual=Person without sexual feelings/desires.
And/Or
Ally=Someone who is educated about the Rainbow and speaks up for this community.

+=Any other colors along the Rainbow Spectrum

Another more memorable, but kinda awkward-sounding option:

QUILTBAG

Which includes all of the above in a convenient word satchel.

Whether it's LGBTQIA+ or QUILTBAG
or a refusal to ascribe any labels at all

I wish I'd known about all the colors

Named and Unnamed

so I wasn't confined to ideas and images and examples
that were so Straight and Narrow.

61

I wish I'd heard more about how people feel

how people love each other

how people identify

and how fluid and flexible
it all can be.

TENTATIVE

I plunge into the swirl of
students

pooling and spinning
laughing and calling

arms locked heads high
gobbling up nutrition break

I scan the slamming lockers
and the girl packs

knowing

words are being whispered
or spoken full-throated

about ME

About my mom
About Sharon

And there's nothing I can do
but try to get to my friends

first.

And...

Oh God

What do I do about Jack?

A Shift of Priorities

I can't think of Jack right now
~of how I pincurled my hair last night
to make some attempt at fullness
of how I broke the rules and put on makeup
that has all been cried off~
because today

TODAY

was the day he was supposed to ask
~since it wasn't yesterday, or the day before that~

either
Me
or
Leyla the Beautiful
to go with him.

I can't think of Jack
I need to tell other people first

relieve myself of this secret
that is no longer secret.

My friends
who I hope will stay true.

My friends
who I realize now

I dearly need
more than any boyfriend.

OUT OF BODY

I'm not sure how I can feel
both in a fog
and
like my vision
~usually blurry because I refuse
to wear my glasses anywhere but in class~
is for once crystal clear

but somehow
that's what it feels like right now
as my world is upended
like some dining room table
in a Mafia movie.

I am flush with panic
hot with fear
charged by an urgent
can-not wait need:

Tell my new friends
before someone else
gets to them first.

I don't know how
the word has gotten out
who it was
or how it could have happened
Today Of All Days.

I plunge into the barren concrete valley
between classrooms.
Across the blurred gray expanse
I see someone shaped like Emma
and I sprint over the concrete
toward her and some girls I'm not close to.

Breathless, chest heaving:
"Can I talk to you for a sec?"

Emma looks surprised
and I am pretty sure she hasn't heard
whatever it is that people are saying.

Her friends move away
with turned-back heads
and I wait until they are out of earshot.

"Look, I—uh—"
—deep rattling inhale—
"There's some rumors okay?
I wanted to tell you myself—umm—
before you hear something from someone else
or something that is not true, okay?"

Emma stares at me
her eyes moving from my eyes to my mouth
my eyes searching hers.

I plow ahead and truth rushes out:

"Look, my mom is gay
she's in a relationship with Sharon
they've been together for like five or six years
she's like my other mom."

Emma's mouth falls open, she gapes for a second.
I can see the wheels spinning on her pretty face.
I can see she is trying to form some appropriate thing to say.

I can see she is lost.
It only takes a microsecond, but it feels like forever.
Something inside me makes the next words come out:

"It—it doesn't mean I'm gay."

It feels like knives stabbing my gut to say it.

Here it is, the Truth:
I am ashamed of my mom and Sharon
I don't want to be like *them*.
There is no way around it.

All I want is to fit in.
Be Normal.

Emma pulls herself together, stammers:
"I—I—don't care it's fine, don't worry."

I can't stay to get more reassurance.
I grab her in a quick hug that feels
desperate and pathetic and needy.

I try to keep the tears back
biting my lip
as I feel her sleek long hair
against my cheek.

It is a super quick hug
that contains the awful thought
that it may be the last we'll ever exchange.

And
then

                    I

                              am

                                             off.

Fighting Wildfire

The rumor is fire
the people are brush
so dry, so ready
and I try to douse the borders
of this barren place
with the hush wave of truth.
Try to stamp out
the flame-bursts of gossip
twisted by someone else's tongue.

I tell:
Emma (who I tell to tell Vivienne)
then I run and tell
        Amy
                Carrie
                        Georgia
                                Debbie

All of them in the first seven minutes of nutrition break.

I am trying to spread the truth
faster than the twisted tale
others may be telling.

Trying to outrace the fire.

You know Sharon?
She's my mom's girlfriend— She's like my other mom—
My mom is gay—They've been together since I was six—
It's no big deal—It's like she's my stepmom—
I hope you don't think it's a big deal—

It Doesn't Make Me Gay—

After I get to all of them
I race back to the bathroom.

I Don't Tell Them What It's Really Like

How Sharon makes my mom laugh

how they hug, kiss, call each other "sweetie-pie"
and "my Quonset Hut of Love"
(*What's a Quonset hut again? An army hut? Huh?*)

how we have family meetings
and they listen to my feelings

how when I told them, carefully
so as not to insult them
that I thought I might be straight
they howled with laughter and said:
"Haze, you're what we gays call a flaming heterosexual."

how Sharon can diffuse any too-tense situation with a joke
how wise she can be

how they snap at each other sometimes
and I want to crawl away

how they like to torture me sometimes
when we're in the car and I'm trapped
they'll sing in unison that whiney song
from forever ago
about following true love
staying loyal no matter where it leads.

How they show me what true love is.

WHERE I'D HOPED TO BE

Hanging on the quad
surrounded by friends
who didn't know my secret
and didn't need to.

Jack and his group nearby
the moment when he
would slide off the fence rail
kick the blond wave off his forehead
and stroll
over to me

give a little chin nod
of invitation
and I'd peel off from my group
run my hands through
my pin-curled hair
and walk away
all those eyes at our backs
warm and knowing
in a good-knowing way

as we stepped into a
new world together.

I imagine the shivery heaven
of those moments before
when we both knew
what words
were to come.

WHERE I AM

Nutrition break
is barely half over.

I close myself
behind the graffiti-scratched stall door

~a tiny crappy closet for the me
who wishes my family was still in one~

put down a chunk of seat covers
sit my best not-Guess jeans on the toilet

and huddle over my knees
to let the tears come.

Seven minutes is a long time
to sob silently

so no one knows.

A Note from your Author:

Bathrooms are crappy places to cry
even with their access to tissue.

What I wish I'd known:
A smidge of Queer Theory.

Heteronormativity: *Noun:* The social construct that says
heterosexuality is normal and everything else is abnormal.

Heteronormativity is reflected in everything: movies and shows
and ads we see all around us, spotlighting one kind of loving:
one masculine man, one feminine woman
one particular flavor of romantic relationships.

In moments like this, when 11-year-old me was huddled
in a shame pool atop seat covers, it would have helped to know
about the rainbow that offers more space, more options
for how you identify, who you love, and how you love.

THEN

The end-of-nutrition bell rings.

The sound of feet scuffing
the stained stupid tile.

The snatches of conversation gathering
then fading away.

I am alone.

I have always been alone.

I imagine rain falling
water upon water
torrents
that might wash
me
and
my salt tears
and this scorched earth

away.

Might cool the world
after all these flames.

AND THEN

I

wait.

And

cry.

Passing period: six minutes.

I

wait.

And

cry.

The tardy bell rings.

I

wait.

Take deep breaths.

And cry all over again.

Until I have that sobbing headache
that comes from so many tears.

Until I have that jagged breath
that comes from too many tears.

As if my body is shaking me to stop
from the inside.

Coming Out

of my closet-
stall into the dimness
of the empty bathroom

tall ceiling
open windows that yawn inward like
gasping mouths: *did you hear?*

the aluminum-cast mirror
making the room even more gray than
it already is

my face crimson blotched
my eyes bluer than usual
thanks to all the red of my skin

my eyelashes clumped and dark
tears the only mascara I am allowed
my whole body in lower-case slump

I look into mirror and think
that this is what it looks like to lose
everything

CRACKED AND CRUMBLED

the foundation of my life
has collapsed

my family
my safety
my home

gone

the guy I like
probably gone soon
if he isn't already

my friends—
who knows?
will they really
stand by me?
are they as good
as their word?
or did they all:

Emma
       Amy
              Carrie
                     Georgia
                           Debbie

lie to me
when they said
they would still
be my friend?

did they
lie to me
as I did to them?

did they

lie to me
as I have lied
to myself

told myself
I wasn't ashamed

when that is
exactly
what I was?

DEEP BREATHS

At the sink:
press the faucet for water
splash my face
and feel the cool
meet the fire.

I press and splash
press and splash
until my face fades
from crimson to pink.

I try to hold on to the
blueness of my eyes
the trade-off
for so many tears.

I still try to find the
Pretty
in the girl who
stares back at me

totally changed.

I can't see it.

It's not there

and it never will be.

MIDDLE SCHOOL HOMOPHOBIA

In this dim pink-tiled bathroom
I think of what I've learned
about middle school and gay people.

In middle school, gay is insult.
Gay is closeted, hidden, secret, silent, shameful.
A perverted choice, some think
not something you are born being
that you can't change, and shouldn't have to.

Ms. Cory, whom I adore, teaches PE
which means she has to be a *Lesbo*.
Maybe she is.
She looks like she could show up at our house
for Thanksgiving in Bermuda shorts and tennis shoes
with all the other lesbians my moms are friends with.

She has short dark hair clunky glasses and a stocky build
maybe not so into her clothes like other women.
But then again, she is a PE teacher
out there with us on the blacktop under the hot sun.
What else should she wear?
She is funny and sometimes sarcastic
quick with praise that ratatatats like staccato chords on a piano.
"Go Kight go go go move move move!"
"That's right girls, pass, pass, pass, you can do it!"

My gut tightens when I hear people speculate about Ms. Cory.
She's totally a Lesbo!
Sometimes I try to say, *"So what if she is?"*
but the words get caught in my throat.
What if people can read my mind?
What if they can tell I'm thinking about
whether my mom's high school students think Ms. Kight
is a *Lesbo*, with her short hair, glasses, and preference for pants.

Talk about gay people
and not-gay people who get called gay
because it's an insult is

all   OVER   Middle   School.

I hear "That's so gay"
ricochet through the halls
many times a day.

It always hurts my heart
when I turn to see who said the words
"You're gay!" or "Homo!" or "Fag!"
and maybe the worst "You have AIDS!!"
and it's someone I *know*.

Someone I used to like.
Someone I pretend I still do.

Even though, I hate to admit
I've used some of those words myself
once, maybe twice.

They tasted like after-throw-up mouth.
They tasted like asphalt, like copper-penny-blood.

All my cells turned to look at me
with the same look I wish I could allow in the halls:

"So, you're *that* kind of person?"

It is so hard figure out where I stand.
The secret inside me puts me one place
the lie to the outside world in another.

The constant trying to spin a different truth inside:

it is a daily battle.

A Note from your Author:

What I wish I'd known:
A smidge more of Queer Theory.

Theorists like Judith Butler (a professor at UC Berkeley)
say sexuality is socially constructed.
Meaning built by society.

Previous theories of sexuality were a cause-and-effect chain,
one idea pointing to the next, in a linear fashion:

"You have a fixed sex (male/female)
you are born with."→

"Culture builds upon this a stable gender
(masculine / feminine)."→

"This gender dictates your desires
(to "opposite" or "same" sex)."

Instead, Butler frames ideas around bodies and identities and desires *without* arrows pointing from one to another:

"You have a body.
You may perform an identity.
You may have desires."

None of these ideas
are dependent upon one another.

None of them are fixed.

They can change
throughout your lifetime.

How liberating.

AIDS, a Personal History

It was back in elementary school, that safe little paradise, so controlled and contained, with kids who didn't know what gay was, and didn't care who your family was, just whether you were a good pick for kickball. (Which I *was* if you wanted a runner but *wasn't* if you wanted a kicker or thrower or someone who'd catch the ball instead of closing her eyes.)

I remember sitting at the table in our old, unremodeled house, as the teeny-tiny kitchen TV chattered evening news, news I usually ignored while deep in some horse book or kid detective tale.

But one night, the anchorman launched the lead story: AIDS, a new disease infecting gay people. At those words, I put down whatever book I was in and looked up at the itty bitty screen, and my insides froze. I listened to the story, about the mysterious disease that was afflicting gay men in New York and other places across the country.

Later, when Sharon wasn't around, I asked my mom: "Are you going to get AIDS too?"

She was quick to reassure me, "No, no, honey. I'm not getting AIDS, neither is Sharon, none of us are."

A wash of cool relief at this, but also hot guilt about the relief. The awfulness of being relieved that I wasn't like *those* people, they weren't like *us*. I wouldn't get sick, but the wondering, too: *How could she be sure?*

There was a boy named Ryan White from Indiana who got AIDS from a blood transfusion. When he tried to return to middle school, parents and teachers were so concerned that he might infect others that they petitioned and protested his return.

Doctors had only given Ryan six months to live, but he managed to live five years longer, and made some famous friends who stood up for him, like Michael Jackson and Elton John.

He caught the attention and sympathy of the nation, in part, it felt like, because he *wasn't* gay. Like that meant it was extra sad he had AIDS. Like he didn't deserve it. Like gay people did.

People did not understand where AIDS came from, how you caught it, or what you could do about it. Kids just knew it as a "gay disease."

And I, with my gay mom, couldn't help but feel a little infected.

WHO

As the panic subsides to crackle-static
in the Period 3 emptiness of the bathroom
I turn my mind to the question:
Who could have told? and *Why*?

Worse still: what does it say about
what people really think about you
if they offer up your secret behind your back
when they were so cool with it to your face?

The possible suspects are still just the four:

Samantha who I hug and hang with, but who I can tell is doing
the math of middle school popularity
and I'm coming up short, so familiar and sister-like, I'm boring.
But I don't think she'd use my secret as currency
in The Quest for Cool. Our moms are still best friends.
I think it's almost like her own secret now.

Ruby, who has made some new friends.
I don't go to her house after school
so we don't really hang out now.
But that's okay. I don't think she would tell.
There's an honor to Ruby, an integrity. She's not a gossip.

Marie is somewhere else, a private school maybe?
She's probably forgotten me as much as I've forgotten her.

And then there's Natalie.
She and I don't hang out much at all.
She's usually in the mix of some popular girls
though I am not quite sure why.
She looks at people with a twist of sour judgment.
She is kind of a Mean Girl sometimes.

A knot tightens in my stomach.

FLEETING

It was a rare event, having people over.

It was always too anxiety-churning to figure out how to explain Sharon, how to act around her so friends didn't know.

I had people over for birthday parties, and Sam came over to play, sometimes Ruby, but not many others.

There was the party in fourth grade where Sharon wrote clues for a treasure hunt that sent our two groups scurrying around the house and backyard looking for clues trying to solve the mystery, just like in my Nancy Drews and my Trixie Beldens. It was so much fun, and everyone was excited, and I didn't feel like I had to explain Sharon at all—she was just the architect of that great day.

It was a rainy afternoon in the middle of fifth grade when Natalie and Ruby came over. And since I didn't want to hang out inside the house with Sharon to explain, or hang out in the rain, I took them to the garage, which was empty of cars, just a wide-open smooth concrete space.

We got the flat dolly that my mom used to move heavy things. It had four planks that formed a rectangle, carpet cushioning the end planks, with an open space in the middle and four wheels, one at each corner. There was a rope connected to the front of it for pulling.

We spun and spun each other till we were all dizzy and then we spun some more. We closed the big garage door and turned off the lights and spun again, this time just a sliver of light coming in, glinting off shiny surfaces, and the sound: rain popcorn-popping down outside, a wall of water as the wheels rattled in circles upon circles, carving infinities on the floor, damp seeping in under the door, and we were together in a warm dark space that hummed with dizzy magic.

After we had our fill of the rattling wheels and the thrill of spin and the laughter that rang out in our little cave, we opened the garage door to watch the wall of the world, the water falling from the sky, silver drops into gray pools, and that smell that comes with rain: wet concrete, wet leaves, wet earth. Damp dirt and everything coming clean.

Which was probably why I decided to. Natalie didn't yet know about Sharon, at least as far as I knew.

But in the otherworldness of the rain and thunder outside, in the giddy high of our fresh-spun selves, I decided to trust her. I decided to tell my secret. Something from our spinning made me want to deepen the closeness that our afternoon had brought. What better way to do that then by telling my secret?

Sitting there, cross-legged on cold concrete, close-leaning in the dark, us three girls creating a circle of confidants, unfolding this truth I sometimes wished wasn't true.

It was different than before.

For the first time, telling felt like a kind of Power.

Hindsight

I wish my real eyes were as good as my hindsight.

I think back on that rainy day

that dizzy spinning
that secret spilling

that thinking I was safe.

What a fool I was.

PRIDE MEMORY

I wait until I am not quite so close to falling apart again.
I try deep breaths, counting to ten
splashing water on my face again.

And in the waiting swirl images:
My mom and Sharon
the Parade of Gay Pride
where we didn't have to hide.
How we lined Santa Monica Boulevard
me in my rainbow shirt, turquoise shorts
all of us standing together, cheering together.

The parade itself: pure spectacle.
Beautiful shirtless muscled men
cowboy hats and short shorts
beaded leather boots, prancing, strutting, swinging
atop a western float, lassoing the crowd.
Women revving bikes in their leather chaps
leather vests, handkerchief headwraps
fists pumping the air.
How they called *themselves* Dykes!
They owned a name that was meant to be an insult.

So many bright shouting colors
cries, whoops, whistles, songs, chants, drums, stomps.
A cornucopia cacophony, raucous riotous rapture
a sense of being part of something beautiful, bright, sweet.
Something that did not need to be hidden
but deserved to be celebrated, honored, cherished.
A protest against confines of closet.

I splash water on my face
remember flags and beads and candy
music blasting into the renegade sun.

I saw other kids with their same-sex parents

and we looked each other in the eye
knowing there was somewhere and someone
with whom we belonged.
That this explosion of joy and hope and pride
was something we were a part of.

All around me, on foot, on motorcycles
on bikes, on fine-flowered floats
my community, my home life, my Secret
was open-aired to the rainbow sky
and there was no hiding, only celebrating.

Somewhere deep and far and cool-quiet
I can still feel the pulse of that parade.
A world where we are normal.

NO~better than normal.
A world where we are *beautiful*.

Hiding in this stupid pink-tiled girls' bathroom
I can still feel the pulse, but it is different now.
It is laced by the sharp edges of truth.

That parade was a lie.
A dream.
The world
the real world
the one I have to live in
doesn't see us as beautiful.

And I can't stand for the world to see me
to see *us*, as ugly.

Better to not be seen at all.

Re-emerging

I step into the quiet chill.

Period 3

the hang-time of day.

Empty halls
closed classrooms.

The leaf-fall of litter
swirling the pavement.

Putty-colored lockers
all slammed shut.

I am forgotten.

It feels like that Twilight Zone
Sharon and I watched together
the one where the people-hating pilot's plane
crashes into desert
and he gets out
and his glasses break
and he realizes he is alone
and he realizes
he really does need people

now that it's too late.

The difference is
I always knew I needed people

and I know
what I am now

going to miss.

Period 3: Tardy

I slouch into
Ms. Feuerstein's math class.
She is mid-lesson
and I slip over to my seat
hoping she doesn't
say anything.

She's one of my favorite teachers
and she must
sense the woe
wafting off me.

She waits until everyone is
working on the even problems, 2-24
to give me a
little questioning glance.

I slide my eyes away and
try to lose myself
in problems
not of my own creation.

The math problems swim
before me
the positives
and negatives

and all those
unequal equations.

PRE-PERIOD 4: WONDERING

At break between
the Math-Science block

I wait as most people leave the class
to head out to the gossip grounds
and catch their six minutes of social.

The weight of wondering so heavy
the pulse of imagining my name spoken
the wildfire of whispers that scorch
even if I am not near.

Shame searing my cheeks
again as I imagine:

"Did you hear about Hazel?"

"Her mom's a lesbian!"

"Can you believe it? That's so gross!"

"Ech, I'm not surprised…"

WHAT are they saying about me?

Wondering whether Jack has heard yet.

Wondering will he be like one of those
characters in the after-school specials

who stands up for what's right, picks the right girl
even after the awful shameful horrible rumors

are found to be true?

Pre-Period 4: A Reprieve

Emma and Vivienne come over
to my seat, where I huddle over my latest Trixie Belden
even though I am just falling into
the spaces between words.

Emma slides into the seat in front of me
Vivienne stands next to my desk
and suddenly I feel buffeted
by these two true friends.

They do not say anything
about what I told Emma, what I told her to tell Vivienne.
They make harmless jokes
about things that I don't even catch

but I fall into the rhythm of their words
and laugh with them
a sweet sad harmony
rising from the low octaves of this day.

They say nothing
of what happened at nutrition
what news was no doubt spread
what may have reached them.

I imagine them at the center of eyes
these two that others know know me
I hate thinking they too
had to ward off the rumors, the scandal.

I wonder briefly~

Would they clarify any confusion?
Would they say "Yeah, I know, so what?"
What did they do when handed my story
dry kindling to stoke gossip flames?

Distant Lands

At lunch I sit on the shallow stairs by the rec room
crunch carrots that taste like sawdust
surrounded by people I've never eaten with before.
I don't want to talk anymore.

Let's face it: I am a coward.
I want nothing to do with battles.

I do not have any desire for confrontation, never have.
I was born into the role of peacemaker with
my mom and dad at war when I was so young.

I want to be around people
that may not have felt the heat of fiery gossip
all my friends must be charred by.

I cannot risk running into Leyla or Leyla's friends:
Surly Girl with sidekicks Smirk Sister and Sour Pout.

That posse of Mean
with their judgment and raised eyebrows.

And most of all:
I cannot risk running into
Jack.

It is like taking a personal timeout from the game.
My head hurts.
White flags of surrender flutter in my mind
like the one waved by the flattened coyote in cartoons.

I tell myself the last thing
I care about now is who Jack picks.

I crunch my carrots and try to
lie to myself as well as I do to others.

BATTLE AVOIDANCE: AN HISTORICAL SNAPSHOT

This I know about myself:
when it comes to Battles and Secrets
I am a stomach-churning mess.
I avoid one and clutch tightly to the other.

I think back to that one day, back in the fall
Back when my secret was still safe.
I left the locker room, stepped into the sloping shadows of 9am
find Surly Girl and her crew gathered at the handball courts.

Surly Girl is a fighter.
Worse still, she's an epic manipulator
who orchestrates fights like some Mean Girl PuppetMaster.
I don't even know how she chooses her victims.

There are all kinds of fights
she brews between people
with her gossip-churning, rumor-spreading, sinister instigations:
"I heard you said Bianca is a two-timing bitch."

And that day, back in the fall
Surly Girl and her posse of Mean were all staring at Me.

Surly was at the center of her pack
maybe five or six other girls gathered around
like she was some kind of mob boss putting out a hit.

I was wishing I had first period P.E. instead of second.
I tried to change my trajectory
but she held me with her stare, did the chin thrust thing
to confirm her purpose, called me over: "Hey. Hazel."

For a second I wondered if maybe I was not the target
but then I saw Dana next to her, staring dead at me.
Dana, a pretty girl with tan skin, taller than Surly, about my size.
Nice sometimes, but with an edge.

Someone I had no interest in crossing.
Surly said, "I heard you were talking smack about Dana, here."

My mouth dropped open.
I hadn't said *anything* about Dana.
To *anyone*. *Ever*.
All the girls had their hands on their hips, ready to attack.

"I never said anything about Dana. Ever."

My stupid voice trembled with fear.
I wanted to run.
My neck felt cold, and I understood about beads of sweat
how they can break out when you are scared.

Surly looked at me, rolled her eyes
pooched her lips out with a sour pout
switched the cock of her hip, sawed her jaw back and forth.
"That's not what I heard."

I looked for an ally, but there was no one.
No one to have my back.
I was on my own.
Trapped by a handball court of girl-hate.

My move. I tried to sound not-scared.
I tried to make my voice strong.

"I swear. I didn't say anything about Dana.
I don't have any problem with her. I like her. She's nice."

I looked at them.
None of them are nice.
They are out for blood.

"I don't want to fight."

That, instead of "I'm not going to fight," which was the truth.

Surly Girl twitched her nose like a bad-witch version
of the mom from *Bewitched.*
She looked like I spoiled her breakfast.
She looked me down and up, slow
from my dirty white Keds to my slouch socks to my bare knees
to my blue PE shorts, rumpled PE shirt
hanging against my flat chest.

Finally she landed at my face
framed by blond wisps that had abandoned my ponytail.

I could tell by that look she was letting me go.
I could tell she had sized me up
and decided I was insignificant, irrelevant
not worth the bother.

I was dismissed with the same chin thrust I was beckoned with.

I veered off alone, shaking
wishing that I had enough courage
to call Surly on her nonsense
wishing I could hold on to my belief:
that fighting was pointless and nothing to seek out.

That not-fighting didn't make me coward.

But somehow it felt like I had failed a test.
And Surly Girl, the most popular
most feared girl in sixth grade
would never again see me as relevant.

And after today, I doubt anyone else will either.

Unless… *Oh God.*

Will a fight solve all of this?

Period 5: Wasted

I head to Ms. Reed's English class
and try not to meet eyes.

Try to make myself invisible.
The food and the juice have
made me feel
a little more human again
but they don't make me feel brave.

They don't transform me
into someone who can hold her head up
walking through this charred, barren wasteland of middle school.

I slide into my seat
and some place inside me *knows*:

Jack asked Leyla to go with him at lunch.

Something in me knows
with such certainty

there is no room for wondering
no room for doubt.

But I am so tired
so wrung dry
I cannot muster much more than a dull ache
as I contemplate

all this day was meant to be

and all it became.

PERIOD 6: BATTLE PLANNING

It's the last slow crawl of the day,
still in Ms. Reed's class, now History
Mesopotamia and the Tigris-Euphrates.

I am thinking of after school
and the confrontation
I know must come.

I am rehearsing what I will say
when I find Natalie
and get the truth from her.

I have pooled what little intelligence
I could from the day
narrowed my suspects down to her.

I know Samantha would never do this
I know Ruby wouldn't either

I know Natalie would

especially to have
fresh currency
with her new friend group.

I am thinking about my opening line
debating whether I have it in me to slap her
whether that would be the right move

when, just then

Jamie Allay

appears in the doorway.

JAMIE ALLAY SAVES THE DAY

Jamie Allay, friend of Kate's sister
is my eighth grade sistergirlcrush
pretty tall thin blond
sleepy blue eyes that exude a sexiness
most middle school girls haven't mastered.
A coolness too, like not much impresses or excites her.

I am semi-obsessed with her
and now she stands at the doorway
and looks right at me
slight raise of the eyebrow
before walking to Ms. Reed
and handing her a golden summons.

Ms. Reed glances down at it
and then up at me. "Hazel?"

She waves the golden paper
as way of explanation
and adds, "Mr. Ollie's office."

I slide out of my seat and wonder
what does the Vice Principal want with me?
Could he possibly know something
about the hell of this day?
Does he have Natalie up there?

Jamie gives me a little smile
as I take the golden pass from Ms. Reed
and follow her out the door.

As soon as we step outside
and beyond view of the class
she turns to me and says:

"I summoned you."

SUMMONED

My mouth and eyes widen
I stare at her sleepy eyes
that now seem to have a bit more spark.

I don't want this moment to end.
Jamie Allay has snuck me out of class.

"I heard something today, and I was worried about you.
I wanted to check and see if you are okay."

I fumble for words: what do I say?
I am standing at the center of Jamie Allay's attention
one of the coolest girls I know is worried about *me*.

"Yeah, um…I…what did you hear?"

"I heard that your mom's boyfriend, you know
messed with you."

My mouth drops, my brain scrambling for sense.

"What? No, that's not true at all."

A flash of disappointment crosses her face
and I rush to clarify, and it all comes out
smooth now after so many raw tellings:

"My mom is gay. She has a girlfriend who is like my other mom."

"Oh." A flicker crosses her face, a new horror occurs to her.

I hurry: "Sharon's never messed with me.
She's great. She's—like my other mom."

Her brow relaxes, "Oh. Ok. That's cool."

"Where'd you hear that other stuff?"

"Oh, you know, people talk, I guess it gets twisted.
You know how it is."

"Yeah." I know how it is.

"Well anyway, I wrote you a note.
I wanted to see if you were okay, so here."

She hands me a square of paper with triangle folds tucked into
each other on one side, like arms tucked in a paper hug.

Then she opens her arms and pulls me in
I press into her tall thin Jamie Allay-ness
smelling her Obsession perfume
feeling the jut of her collarbone
against my cheek.

She came to see if I was okay.
She got me out of class.

I can't believe how a day so awful could give way to this:

Me, in Jamie Allay's arms
her wanting me to feel better
enough to write me a note, fold it sweet
bust me out of class
and hold me for a moment.

Something about her view from eighth grade
makes me step outside
of the squeezed-tinytight-awful of my day
and makes me think

somehow I'll be okay.

THE NOTE

I slide back into my seat
after my conference with Jamie Allay
still feeling the thrill of her eyes on me
the comfort of her arms
like I just got to experience
what an older sister at my school
might really be like.

I tuck behind my history book
and unfold the interlocking triangles
at the back of the note
and untwist the angles of it
until it is one long snake of
white and blue lines

unfold further
until the two pages are open
in their creases and complexities
hoping I can recreate the twists
to figure out how
to fold notes like this.

I look at her perfect blue letters
and dive into the words
Jamie Allay has crafted
just for me.

She tells me some of the things she told me outside:

How she wanted to make sure
I was okay, because
~and here, she added things she hadn't said outside~
there was a time
when she went through something awful too
with her mom's boyfriend
and him messing with her

and it screwed her up
for a long time
and she thinks that's why
she sort of hates her body
and she wants me to know
that I can talk to her
Anytime about Anything.

I glance up at Ms. Reed
to make sure she doesn't see
and look down again at the note
reread the part about Jamie's mom's boyfriend
look again at the hearts
in her signed name.

Wonder if she knows
how much I have looked up to her
watched her, wanted to be her.

It makes me feel strong, cared about
by one of the coolest, prettiest eighth graders
at our school.

I feel like I have a guardian angel.

I reread the note until
I know it well enough
to pass a quiz on it

and I feel something in me

sprout to life

from the ruin
of this long day.

THE RUINS

My eyes scan the history book
so many ancient stories of relics and ruins, battles and wars.
My pen doodles the edge of my notebook
my own history with ruins a faint memory from six years ago.

On the island my dad and I used to walk every day
sometimes along the overgrown path beside
fields that veered to the left
down the hill that swooped toward the valley below.
Suki the dog bounding ahead in her eternal hunt
for a rabbit she could catch.

We walked through the tall blond grass
stepping with care to avoiding rabbit holes
that could twist an ankle good.

Down the hill, past the woods, under a blue or gray sky
until we came to the Ruins.

They jutted haphazard to the sky
things both familiar and foreign in their disintegration
the cinderblock foundation of a once-house.

We walked around the inside of once-rooms
and I imagined walls with wallpaper, pictures hanging
sofas where someone stretched out to nap.
The burnt-out old stove where maybe the fatal fire started?

Rusted out pipes, jagged half-walls.
Half-squares where windows had been
where I could look out at a once-view
wider now with the roof gone:
the sloping valley, the far-off farmhouses and barns and fields
bales of hay that sat in giant rolls or big-bricked stacks.

A place some family once watched the world

from an inside that no longer was.
There was something awful-beautiful in those ruins
something that spoke of a life that was now lost.

The burning of a home, of a history.
It was terrifying and intriguing all at once.

As I huddle in the ruins of my day, of my secret
I remember that early spring we walked again to the ruins
a morning when the eagles were storying the sky overhead
Suki bounding off after those elusive rabbits.

We came down the hill and I saw the flowers:
pale-faced ladies with yellow crowns bowing in the breeze
dressed in thin emerald gowns.
Their arms reaching an embrace toward the sky.
So many daffodils crowded around
the crumbling scarred cinder blocks
the cement foundation
like they had gathered in memorial of what had been.

Like the fire was needed, was vital
in making the earth around those ruins abundant again.

We wandered among the daffodil gatherings
their happy conversing, their elegant manners
and maybe my dad was quieted by the loveliness
or maybe I didn't notice his always-words.

Maybe, as so often happened on the Island
when we walked that land
we were connected by something deeper than words.

Maybe we saw what glory can arise amid ruin
and there was nothing that needed to be said.

Dismissal: What Is Known

I decide that when the bell rings
I have to make a stand.

I know who it is.

I rehearse my lines
again and again in my head
as Ms. Reed talks
fertile valleys and ancient trade routes.

I look around me at my classmates
wondering how many of them heard
something about me today
currency trafficking all those old routes
gossip that may or may not be true.

I wonder how many of them
know how I have been
scorched
ruined
by the wildfire of gossip.
How can they just sit in those seats
with all that has happened?

I wonder if they
are thinking about me at all.
Or if this thing that
feels like a neon billboard on my back
is anything at all?

How much do people think
about other people
when there is so much
thinking to do
about your own
stupid ugly awkward self?

Find Her

The bell rings and some tiny part of me thinks
that in a flip dimension, a Twilight Zone of goodness
I might be finding Jack right now
and getting a hug from the guy who asked me to go with him.

Instead, my biggest concern is finding
Natalie
not Jack.
In fact
I hope I don't see him at all.

I head out into the bright day
the afterschool hustle
of stuffing lockers and slamming metal
sprints and hugs, updates between friends.

I see her
standing under the eave of the hallway
talking to a friend, and I can tell:
she knows I'm coming.

There is a self-consciousness
in the slant of her back
or maybe I'm just imagining it.

Maybe this day has been nothing to her.

I walk toward her
see her long thin
brown ponytail swivel
so that her face turns to me.

"Natalie. I need to talk to you. Alone."

She looks back at her companion
a girl who always has a sour smile for me

who now drifts off with her usual smug attitude
and I can tell Natalie is nervous, trying to compose the lie.

"Sure, what's up?"

She half-turns toward me
like maybe this can all be wrapped up quickly
like she has an important
conversation to get back to.

"Over here."

I lead her into the bright sunlight
her arms folded in front of her body
like she is protecting herself
from the words she knows are coming.

"Did you tell people about my mom?"

Her face registers rehearsed surprise
guilt, uncertainty
maybe an ounce of regret?
Or maybe I'm just being generous.

"I—I might have said something to like, one person."

"Yeah, well, they might have told a few people too.
People I don't even *know* know."

"I—"

"I trusted you. You said you wouldn't tell."

She looks at me with worried blue eyes
and I watch her hands try
to figure out what to do with themselves.
They reach and flutter and do not seem to know
that they are supposed to be denying the whole thing.

"You broke your promise."

Suddenly Surly Girl's drama-driven voice is in my head
"You should slap her. You should fight."

I look at the color already rising on Natalie's face
and I know I can't hit her, no matter what she's done.

Even if she outed my family. Even if she cost me Jack.

Natalie looks at me, says:

"Sorry."

Shoulder shrug, face defensive, pathetic.

I search for words, can only come up with:

"It's not okay."

I keep wishing I could hit her, but I can't.

Instead:

                    I turn my back

                                        and walk away.

THE NEWS

It comes confirmed
through some source
at the end of the day
after the moment with Natalie.

Jack and Leyla
are going together.

Officially.

I think about what Jack
might have heard about me today
What Leyla and Natalie
might have made sure he heard.

I think there's no way Jack
is brave enough
to ask out a girl
whose moms have just been outted
across the school.

He would never take a stand like that.

Or, even worse:
would he, if I was worth it?

I begin

the long

walk home

alone.

THINKING

I walk through the streets

                I've walked my whole life.

Nature blaring brilliance all around

                    I try to find refuge.

There is so much I do not notice

                when walking with someone

or when I'm happy.

                So much I take for granted.

I think about my moms, wish

            I didn't feel so ashamed of them

their secret love something

                others do not want to see.

A tiny flicker of frustration inside:

              why would anyone think love

true, whole-hearted love

             between two people is wrong?

I try to summon the pride of the parade

                  of Thanksgivings

of women gathered in story and laughter

                but it is not there.

I try to remember something

                I might be able to say:

some slogan about the right

             to love whom you choose

something to throw in the faces

           of Natalie / Leyla / Jack / Surly.

Something to shatter

               all their judgment.

But I know:
no matter how pretty
and perfect the words

They will always
prefer judgment.
They feed on it.

It's so delicious, so juicy.
So satisfying, so safe.
So easy, so awful.

So essential
to what being *Cool* means.
And I know I will have to find a way

to choose something else.

ALONE

I open the door to our front yard trailer
not a glance at the progress on our house.
I make my usual microwave popcorn
but today it tastes like charcoal.

When my mom
and Sharon
and Bronja
get home

they say, "Hey, Haze!"
"How was your day?"
and I lie:

"Fine."

All through dinner I stay quiet
locked up inside myself

as the talk swirls around
and past and beyond me.

I marvel at what it is like
to feel so alone

in a trailer full of people
who are supposed to know

when I'm not there.

Part Two:

AfterGrowth

Things I Know Nothing About

I don't know who Harvey Milk was:
that he was openly gay and politically active in San Francisco
that he helped pass laws that protected gay and lesbian people
from losing their jobs to discrimination
and he helped fight a proposal that would make it illegal
for gay folks—like Mom and Sharon—to be teachers.

I don't know that he was killed about a year
after his election to the San Francisco Board of Supervisors:
so much vital work cut short.

I don't know that homosexuality was listed as a mental illness
in the big book of psychiatric disorders—the DSM—
starting in 1952
until finally, twenty years later, a group of gay activists
and a masked psychiatrist
would testify that homosexuality did not make them
—or anyone else—mentally ill.

In 1973, two years before I came along
the American Psychiatric Association bigshots would finally lift
gayness from the list of things that could be wrong with you.

I don't know that once psychiatry legitimizes homosexuality
the Christian Right will step in to take up the torch of bigotry
with gay conversion therapy by a group called "Love in Action"
who "ministers" to people who commit
the "sin" of homosexuality.

The National Institute for Health would later find that people
who went through conversion therapy
were more than twice as likely to attempt suicide.

I don't know that my first Pride parade was
commemorating the Stonewall Uprising
when the gay community in New York City

fought back against police who attacked queer people
at a favorite bar, the Stonewall Inn.

I don't know that AIDS patients in lots of places
couldn't have their partners visit them in hospitals
because they weren't seen as official family.

I only know
growing up
as the child of two moms
in Los Angeles in the 80's

that *gay* is an insult
that *homo* and *fag* and *queer*
are synonyms
for weak and pathetic and perverted.

And that if you try to speak out against this idea
try to say, "So what if someone's gay?"
you'd be shunned, called gay yourself
and that stamp of shame would stick.

And that is enough to make me not want
to go back to school
ever again
after the firestorm

of yesterday.

THINGS MY MOM
KNOWS NOTHING ABOUT

I cannot tell my mom
why I do not want to go to school today.

I cannot tell her about the secret that got out
about my deep wish that it had never gotten out.

My even deeper wish that it didn't have to be true
in the first place.

And the whole-body shame
for those sorry, sad, secret wishes.

My gut is so clenched
I can barely stand my spoonfuls of Raisin Bran.

I retreat into
the bathroom

and try to vanish
into the beige plastic paneling.

Getting Back on the Horse

Hiding in the tiny trailer bathroom, I think about when Mom
used to take my horse-crazy girl-self to riding lessons.
My first lesson horse was named Yankee
a chestnut with a white blaze down his nose.

One day Martina, the Austrian horse trainer lady
with the German accent and the strict way of teaching
had me posting around the ring up down, up down.

As we rounded the far curve, Yankee spooked
and a shuddering horse earthquake erupted under me.
I tightened my whole body, bent low over his neck
and *Oh God Oh God* ripped through my bone-shaking terror.

We raced down the long side of the ring
and just as we rounded the near curve
Yankee planted his feet and STOPPED, but I didn't.

I kept going, in what must have been a lovely arc
of spinning tumbling horse-girl
until I hit that ground hard
breath slammed out of me
and I was staring up into Yankee's flaring nostrils
wondering how I got there
and where my breath had gone.

Martina came over, stuck out her hand to help me up
and said, "You alright?"

"Uh…"

"Good. Deep breaths, dust off, and back up you go."

I gaped my mouth at her
dragged that missing breath back into my body
from wherever it had gone

looked at her, like:
You can't be serious. Did you just see that fall?

She turned her back, walked to Yankee,
grabbed the reins as he pulled his head away
like he knew what was coming
and then she YANKED poor Yankee hard
jerking those leather straps, as he jerked his head
and went all white-eyed in response.
She slapped the meat of his right shoulder
and said some horse curse in German.

He almost looked sorry.

Then to me:

"Ready? Up you go."

And before I knew it
there I was next to Yankee
both of us still catching our breath
bending to the will of that strict lady together.

Inside a minute we were going again
and at the end of the lesson she said:

"Listen: when you've fallen off a horse 100 times
then you'll be a good rider."

And just like that: a complete reframing of my fears of falling.

Falling didn't mean failing.
Falling meant learning.

Get back on the horse.

How simple it is
when you're just talking about horses.

RETURN

I slide in next to Sharon and the whole drive I feel numb
like I am a thousand miles from the world
passing outside the windows.

I replay yesterday, what I said, and what I didn't.
I may have said the words, "My mom is gay"
but how could I describe what it means to have two moms?

That there's lots of listening when I need it.
Too many family meetings when I don't.
That they don't hold hands in public
or show each other much affection out in the world.

Only sometimes, when the place is really safe
do they put their arms around each other, sometimes kiss
and I guess like any kid seeing their parents
do that kind of thing, it's a little gross.

There is safety in cars, in the place that used to be our house.
There is safety at other women's houses
with other families that are sort of like ours.

They embarrass me. Occasionally torment me.
They do the same things other parents do, I guess.
There's no "I'll talk to your father"
instead, there's more of a "We'll have to talk about it."

They are a team.
I guess they are pretty good parents.
Too bad I can't talk to them about any of this.

I scramble out when Sharon pulls over by the side gate
say a quick "Goodbye, thanks, have a nice day."

Slam the door fast,
shoulder my backpack and head into the fray.

LEYLA AND JACK

This is how bad it is:
I hope the talk will be about them
not about me.

And there, in the distance
across the concrete valley

Jack and Leyla.

His arm cool casual
around her shoulder
like she has always been a part of him
like she is *his*.

His blond hair swoops
her thick black waves whoosh.

Their eyes shining and full
of this thing glowing between them.

It could have been me.

I imagine the weight of his arm
the press of the side of his body against mine

steering through the world
together.

INSTEAD

The yawning ache inside.
That feeling of not being picked.
A thousand times worse than not being picked for kickball.

The whispers crackling through morning mist
rumors rustling in early breeze
secrets sliding through middle school currents.

Still, I imagine, about me
my moms, those *Lesbos*.

I head toward my friends.
Those who heard my confession yesterday
and pardoned me.

I try to forget that yesterday
was the worst day
of my life.

I try to forget about

whispers
and
rumors

secrets
and
shame

lies
and
rejection.

JENNY'S WORDS OF WISDOM

Jenny: fearless, funny, sharp-tongued girl, Iris's friend
curly-haired, cute clothes, cutting edge of every trend

has this thing that I heard her say once
that has stuck with me
even as I can't quite figure out
how to embrace it.

"If I laugh at my own haircut
or point out my ripped sweatshirt
before someone else does
what can they say?

It's not like they're telling me
something I don't already know."

My brain tries to latch on
to this small bit of brilliance.

If I was into sports
I might know it as
"the best defense is a good offense."

There is something to this
some answer that I need to understand.

But at the same time
it is terrifying to imagine
what this would look like
with the thing I'm most afraid to embrace.

How do I make my family-truth
into a bad-haircut-comment
so no one else can?

MOVING ON

It still hurts
these twin pangs:
the truth about my moms
and
the crush of losing my crush.

Like twin moons
orbiting my gravity.

I try to focus on other things.
Other gossip that is passed at passing time, nutrition, lunch.
Gossip that is about people not me.
Gossip I gobble guiltily, because I know how awful
it feels to be gossiped about, and I know how badly
I want people to talk about anyone other than me.

I try to avoid looking at
Jack or Leyla
but it is hard.
I sneak near-sighted looks around campus
across the lunch quad, in the hallways
watch their blurry coupledom
and wonder how I thought
it could ever be me.

Each time
like tearing off the scab
and feeling fresh raw pain.

I trudge around so heavy
with the weight of these
two things

pulling me down
anchoring me
to Earth.

THE NEWS, PART 2

Days after the wildfire
that burned me to nothing

I learn that Jack and Leyla
have broken up.
It hasn't even been a week.

There's a stupid tiny green tendril of hope
that shoots up from the ash
and whispers pathetic little flutters:

maybe Jack will ask me now.

But I know, even if he did
which I doubt in a million, bazillion years
it's ruined now.

I know who he chose
when he had the chance
to take a stand
and not care that the girl he liked
comes from a family
that's a little bit different.

But deep down, I realize:
maybe that wasn't the deciding factor after all.

Maybe he just liked Leyla more.
I don't know which is worse:
Him not choosing me because my mom's gay, OR
Him not choosing me because he doesn't like me.

I just know that I'm hoping
something new and strong will start growing
on this scorched earth
after all that fire.

TIME LURCHES ALONG

I still don't tell my mom about the wildfire day
I had at school last week.
I don't tell Sharon
I don't even tell Bronja.

If I told them they would know
that the reason I still feel so epically awful
a week later
is because part of me wishes
my mom wasn't gay.

And all of me wishes
I didn't feel that way.

A new secret.

Shame for the shame:
vast, galactic, impossible to hold.

I just want it to go away.
I just want to be *normal*.

I wish I could go back to
when my secret was secret.

Or further still~
to a time when
there were no secrets
and no need for lies
that would one day be exposed.

Did that time ever exist?

Near the End of Dinner

I get up to use the mini-bathroom
that is right next to the kitchen/dining room
the way everything is right next to everything
in this dumb trailer.

While I'm sitting on the half-sized toilet
I look down and do not understand what I see.
Something rust-brown and not normal
and after a couple of hanging-in-midair moments, I know:

Period.
Oh *God…*

I want to twist out of my body
and leave it crumpled on the floor
but there's no room
in this too-small broom closet of a bathroom
this too-small mobile shed of a trailer
this under-construction remodeling of my life.

Sister-not-sister from Germany
two moms instead of a regular mom-dad family
secret I have pounded nails into
slapping onto the sturdy two-by-fours of truth
something fake and sloppy and unstable.

Now this: brown ick on white cotton
splotch of adulthood before me
in a place so unprivate I can still hear every word
of conversation from the dining room half-table
two feet and one thin-ass door away.

I wad up toilet paper and try to wipe it away, but it stays
I wad up toilet paper and press it onto underwear
because I know there is more coming.

I look at myself in the mirror:
those everywhere baby zits on pink skin
those blue eyes that are my only hope at Pretty.

That who-am-I-fooling hair
with the pin-curl waves that always fall out by nutrition.
That little curve on my top lip that my eyes can rest on
tiny life raft on an oil-slick sea.

This month
of all months.

Haven't I had enough humiliation?

COME ON, MOM

I step out of the broom closet bathroom back to cramped table.
Everyone is finishing their food.
I take a deep breath and say:
"Mom, can I talk to you for a minute?"

She looks up, concern on her face. "Sure, Petunia"
and we walk out the narrow door of the trailer
into the cool evening, the sky soft violet
our unfinished house rising above us.

It's the only place that makes sense.
I walk up to our front door and into the
world of fresh wood and see-through walls
the bones of a home
that sprang from so much careful planning.
I stop into our once and future living room.
Turn to her.

"I think I got my period."

She opens her arms, gives the most embarrassing joyful shout:
"I knew it! You're a woman!"
and throws her arms around me
into the most unwanted hug ever
complete with laughter and a little hug-dance.

I C K.

If this is becoming a woman
I'd much rather stay a girl.

If this is sharing the truth
I'd much rather carry the secret.

I look around our once and future living room
and wonder if houses have growing pains too.

Now This

Like every morning
Joe the contractor does his knock-knock on the trailer door
says hello and slides into the bench seat
which, like every morning
is my cue to get up
and go into the bathroom.

But now
there are pads my mom gave me in the little
pencil case cabinet above the sink.
The bag she gave me to take to school.

It feels so awful and obvious between my legs.
Everybody is going to know.

Yet another secret to keep.
More shame to smother.

I turn around and stand tippy-toe
to see my butt through the mirror
try to find the lines
of this new thing
I have to wear.

I hate secrets.
I hate wondering who knows and who doesn't.
I hate wondering who's still talking about the things
I try to keep hidden.

I hate the lies
I may have to tell
to keep all the secrets

Secret.

A Note from your Author:

Yep, three chapters on the unique ick
of getting your period for the first time.

If you get your period, you *get* why this is such a big deal, even if
we do live in a time when getting your period doesn't mean
you are married off to the highest bidder to fulfill
your one function in life, which is to make heirs.

If you don't get a period, and likely will not get a period
because of the fact of the body you were born into:

thank you for spending a tiny fraction of your day
thinking about what it is like to have your body become

a secret blood-making machine several days each month.

Three chapters is just the tip of the iceberg.

NOT SIDEKICK

Jack's Sidekick comes up to me a week or two after all of it.

It's lunch time, a little bird of hope flutters
maybe he brings news:
that since Jack's dumped Leyla
he realizes the awful mistake he's made
that I'm the one, and have always been the one.

I imagine he'll say can I please forgive Jack
for not being there for me
and will I still go with him?

But instead Sidekick, his sweat-slicked nose
causing him to crinkle-scooch his
glasses up every few seconds
asks me, straight to my face
no middle man go-between at all:

"Do you want to go with me?"

I feel sick.

How could he ask me
when Jack was supposed to ask me
and Jack is his best friend?

"Sorry, Sidekick,
I like you as a friend, you know?"

I watch his face flinch, his body squirm
like he's trying to shrug off the question
like he never even asked it.

I feel heavied by this pathetic power I have
to hurt a boy I never wanted to hurt.

A NOTE FROM YOUR AUTHOR:

There's this thing called YouTube.

Pause for a moment.

Search up "Flintstones Kids Vitamin Commercial."

Press play.

Go ahead. The book will be here when you get back.

I'll see you in 30 seconds.

Careful…don't get lost over there.

PUT IN MY PLACE

Fresh off the heels of my Sidekick rejection
that made me feel both a smidge superior and
like the slime of the earth for feeling any kind of superior

I am firmly put in my place:
and it is Nice Guy who starts it.

Sweet, doe-eyed Nice Guy
dark hair, easy smile
so cute, so sweet it would hurt
if he wasn't so short.

Nice, who is friends with Mean Boy.
Nice Guy, who is so Not Mean
who is so sweet, so cute it would hurt
if he wasn't so short.

He's the one.

Passing time
just hanging out, trying to feel at ease again
in the wake of Jack-Letdown Gay-Explosion Period-Arrival
Sidekick-Rejection-Drama

I hear it:

across the dried-up concrete creek bed
between classroom rows
Nice Guy stands with
Mean Boy and Quick Trigger, and sings:

"We are Hazel's zits, 10 million strong and growing..."

sung perfectly to the tune of the
Flintstones Kids Vitamin Jingle, that oh-so-catchy one
sung by a pack of kids in the commercial

all one big happy chorus.

We are Flintstones kids, 10 million strong and growing!

So catchy anyone can sing it.

And now Nice Guy
clearly due for a Name Change

has made that song *mine*
along with my *10 million zits*
all so strong and growing.

Oops

Mr. Laddin's class is my refuge now.

His art class is outlet
for all the middle school mayhem
and I love him and his grump schtick.

Which is why
        I somehow feel comfortable enough
                one morning

when the awfulness of my broken secret
                        still breaks across me every day

        to walk into art class
                and greet Mr. Laddin
                        with a "Hey Laddin!"

and I make my hand
        into a fist
                and sink it
                        along with all my awful outted feelings

>>>SSSMMMMOOOOOSSSSHHHH<<<

into his perfectly round Pillsbury-dough B E L L Y.

        My mind explodes into fireworks of
                NO NO NO STOP STOP STOP
                        WHAT THE HELL ARE YOU DOING???

But it's too late.
My fist punches into his belly
the way my mom used to let me
punch the yeast-huge dough
on Saturday bread-making mornings.

I am consumed by a waterfall of regret
even before I have my fist back.

Mr. Laddin is
not joking
not playing
not pretending
not schticking

when he bellows

"THAT'S IT KIGHT! YOU'RE OUTTA HERE!

GO TO THE OFFICE!"

My favorite stronghold of safety is shattered.

When did I become a girl who *punches teachers*?

Who the hell am I?

Obedience

On the long walk to Mr. Ollie's, I contemplate:

There was a time I won awards for my obedience.
It wasn't that long ago.

We enrolled our exuberant, pound-rescued pup, Cindy
in obedience school at the park
with Mr. Ewing, dog-trainer, owner-trainer extraordinaire.

Cindy and I went every week
she in her choke-chain
me holding the red-brown leather leash
in a loop firm in my right hand
with Cindy on my left
paying perfect attention
to Mr. Ewing's every command.

At first she was spotty at best
but over time she learned
to heel and sit and stay and come.
I learned to *"Praise 'em up, Good dog, Good dog"*
and hold that leash firm.
Cindy and I were a team
and most chilly mornings before school
we were out, practicing on the sidewalk again and again,
so that she would learn and listen and follow my lead.

On the night of the class competition
Cindy nailed the routine
stayed when I told her to
and we took home a trophy as tall as she was.
Obedient champions.

Cindy has grown more obedient with age.

I, apparently, am growing less.

MR. OLLIE'S OFFICE

I walk up to the Vice-Principal's office
and wish it was the period that Jamie Allay
worked in there as a TA.

I could use one of her hugs.

Instead, I walk in with my dread-heavy gut
like I was the one who took a fist to the belly
and not the one with the fist.

Mr. Ollie is sympathetic, maybe even biting back a smile
says he's never heard anything about me before
which means I'm probably a good kid
who never gets in trouble.

Relief seeps in a little at this, and I say:
"I've never been sent to the office before."

He nods, his brown eyes soft.
"Write him a letter of apology
and give it to him tomorrow.
Give him a day to cool down
and I'm sure you'll be able to move past it."

I nod, swallow.

"Do I stay here for the rest of the period?"
Thinking: I don't want to sit with the other kids out there.

But he nods again
and I spend the longest forty-five minutes ever
in that depressing room, writing my apology
trying to get the words right

and trying to forget the feel of Mr. Laddin's soft denim shirt
and poochy dough belly around my fist.

Mr. Ollie was kind in deciding not to suspend me that day.
It wasn't an assault. It was a mistake.

If any adults are reading this:
All kids should get passes like that.

Really.

Our brains are not working right yet.
Give us a break.

Ask us what's going on.
Find out what heartache or horror we are living through.

It'll explain a lot.

You just might remember how hard it is
to be a kid sometimes.

Two Moms Different

Having Bronja around starts to *kind of*
make me see the two moms thing
in a different light.

A distant, light-years from me kind of light.

Bronja seems totally fine with it, happy even.
Like my mom and Sharon are cool for loving each other.
It doesn't seem like something she would worry about
keeping secret.

I wonder:
what does Bronja know about my family that I don't?
What does Sharon share with Bronja
that she doesn't with me?

How she feels about my mom?
How she realized she was a lesbian?

I have a feeling they talk about
Sharon's wild youth
parties concerts drugs
things that she has only hinted at with me.
Like they are more sisters than Bronja and I are.

I don't tell Bronja about the secret
that is out around school about my family.

I don't think she would understand why it is so hard.
She wouldn't understand the Shame I carry around.

The double Shame:
Shame that my mom is gay
that Sharon is my parent

and worse: Shame for the Shame.

A Note from your Author:

What I wish I'd known:
There were lots of queer folk in history, and some of them were
epic rule-breakers, not just convention-testers.

Frida Kahlo was a free-loving painter from Mexico who suffered
a horrific bus accident when she was just a teenager.

Despite 39 surgeries and constant pain, Frida had many lovers,
both male and female over her lifetime. She married the painter
Diego Rivera and had a tumultuous relationship with him as she
established her own artistic life.

Frida gained fame as a painter in her own right, and when she
finally had a solo show in Mexico, doctors forbade her from
getting out of bed due to her poor health.

Frida, never one to follow rules, had herself carried to the show
in her four-poster bed so she could attend.

LONGING

Now that so much has crumbled:

Jack

my Secret

I am left aching
for someone
who is there for me
no matter what.

Someone to share
inside jokes
secret smiles
someone who would've
ditched with me at third period
and smoothed back my hair
as I sobbed in the bathroom stall.

Instead I did that all alone.

Someone better than a foreign exchange sister
someone more like a
real, always-got-your-back sister
a genuine friendship.

A Best Friend.

To be accepted in my entirety:

mom-warts
puberty-skin
insecure-awkwardness
and all.

STANDING UP

I realize one day, as I look around
at the clumps of classmates
the girls gathered with hands on hips
the boys doubled over with laughter

that everything has changed.

From the blackened earth of *that* day
tiny green shoots of something new
are curling out of my charred heart.

I assume everyone knows now.

And it's a surprising form of relief.

If they don't know
I can tell them
or someone else will
either way
I don't feel like I'm carrying a secret anymore.

Just something that is different about me
I get to figure out how to share.

I get to make this story mine
rather than a secret I hope no one finds
and there is Power in that.

And something else I get to figure out:
in the hallway
I hear firecracker-temper Quick Trigger
say "You're so Gay!"
to some boy I don't know.

I look at him, catch his eyes with my stare
knowing his famous short-fuse temper

knowing his tendency to use fists to win fights
and I say:

"You shouldn't say that.
There's nothing wrong with being gay."

His mouth drops open and he fish-gapes
for a moment, wheels turning
trying to figure out what to say.

I wonder if anyone has ever
said these words in the history
of Middle School Hell.

He looks like he has never
thought about the alternative I am presenting:

That gay can be something that is
OK.
Something that is not an insult.

He recovers,
squares his tough-guy shoulders
and I hover
anticipating Quick Trigger's firecracker-temper.

He shrugs and goes with:
"Whatever."

Somewhere
deep inside
my fire-scorched self
underneath the shame
the secret
the hiding

an ally is born.

A Note from your Author:

What I wish I'd known:

Bayard Rustin was a Black man living in the North
who traveled to the segregated South during the early forties.
While riding on a bus a woman called him a racial slur
and initially he moved to the "colored" section of the bus.

Upon reflection, he decided there was no time like the present
to desegregate that public space
so he returned to sit at the front.
The driver told him repeatedly to move
and he refused, later stating:
"My conscience would not allow me to obey an unjust law."

Four police officers beat him for refusing to move
and when he was taken to the station
he demonstrated nonviolence in the face of state violence.

In 1963, Bayard was one of the organizers
of the March on Washington for Jobs and Freedom
a march that drew a quarter million people to DC
where Dr. King shared his dream.

Bayard was often kept in the shadows
despite his vital leadership
for fear his sexuality would delegitimize the movement.

But he was an essential part of the push
for racial justice through nonviolence.

No one throughout my K-12 school years ever taught me
about the queer folk who have made history
who have stood up against injustice.

Not a single one.

FIGHT ORGANIZER STRIKES AGAIN

We are gathered around the side
of the girls' gym one cool spring morning.

Yelling comes from the group near us
and I turn to see Kate and Nina
former Best Friends
squared off, hands on hips
staring at each other as a crowd assembles.

Nina's face is beet-red, eyes tear-full.
Kate is shrugging off some comment from Nina:
"Go ahead and slap me if it'll make you feel better."

And then, so fast I am wondering if it really happened
Nina reaches out and slaps the glasses right off Kate's face.

I see Kate's head snap back from the stun of the slap
her mouth an "O" as color rises on her cheeks like a red tide.

Someone picks up Kate's glasses from where they clattered
across the pavement, and the two are swarmed by the others.

Surly Girl is in the middle of it
looking on with triumphant ugliness
and I know, even before anyone tells me
that she was the instigator of it all.

Amy puts her arm around Kate and they walk off together.

Even though Kate was the one slapped
I think everyone knows she came off better out of the two
a winner without even throwing a return slap.

There's a courage in that that I love:
Holding your head high.
Not slapping back.

BRONJA'S ALWAYS BETTER

Bronja's got a friend, named Belinda.
They hang out a lot
and Belinda seems totally comfortable
with my mom and Sharon
being who they are.

Bronja's junior prom at Culver High
is coming up
and she's decided she wants to go
with Belinda.

She wants her date to be a *girl*.

I can't believe it.

Bronja's so pretty and funny and cute
I'm sure she gets tons of attention
from guys because she's so different
with her cute German accent
short stylish hair
funky homemade clothes
she sews herself.

I'm sure there are plenty of guys
she could go with
but for some reason she's
choosing Belinda.

I don't think she *likes* her likes her
I think they are just friends
I think she's trying to make some kind of statement
in support of my mom and Sharon maybe?

Maybe because she wants to be different
and wear a tux to prom?

I think about the problems
she might be creating for herself:

What if someone doesn't like the statement she's making?
What if she gets hurt?
What if my mom and Sharon
think Bronja supports them more than I do?

What if they think *she*
a temporary add-on to the family
is a better daughter?

What if she is?

A Note from Your Author:

Bronja was playing with gender expectations
with this whole prom plan.

Gender, like sexuality, is also something
a bit more open-ended:
it's not necessarily the same as the gender
you are assigned at birth.
(It's a girl! or It's a boy! Well…Maybe!)

Gender can be fluid.
You may identify anywhere along the range
of masculine to feminine,
and this too may shift over your lifetime.

What I wish I'd known:
Some key terms and ideas…

Cisgender: If you identify with the gender

you are assigned at birth.

Transgender: If you identify with the gender opposite
the one you were assigned at birth.

Non-Binary / GenderQueer / Gender Fluid / Intersex:
If you fall somewhere else, or flow freely
along the spectrum of the masculine/feminine binary.

There's no "right way" to perform your gender identity.

You get to be true to yourself

whoever you are

on any given day

in all your rainbowed complexity.

Dance Practice

Right before spring break
we have a dance scheduled
in the rec room at school.

The night before
while Bronja is visiting with my mom and Sharon
in the back room turned bedroom behind the garage
I listen to my *True Blue* Madonna cassette tape
on my mini mint boombox:
"Papa Don't Preach," "La Isla Bonita."

I try to dance in the cramped space but
all my motions are so awkward and uncertain
I'm certain the neighbors are spying at me and my absurdity.

Like my arms aren't connected to my shoulders
like my legs don't meet up with my hips.
Like all of me is in a dozen pieces
and I have to make them fit together when they don't.

Slow dances I can do. Those are easy.
Girls put their hands on guys' shoulders
and step side to side and back again.
But no one at school is going to ask me to slow dance.

At least I've finally started to feel like the first thing
people think about me when they see me might not be
"Her mom is gay."

I don't know who I'll dance with at the dance.
Definitely not Jack.

But I want to be ready.
Just in case someone asks me.

So, I practice.

DANCE

We pour into the darkened rec room
the milky light glowing from the windows
pooling on the dance floor.
Lots of dark corners to hide in
alone
or with someone else.

They play Madonna's "Open Your Heart"
The Bangles' "Walk Like an Egyptian"
Belinda Carlisle's "Heaven is a Place on Earth"
Club Nouveau's version of "Lean on Me."

My body thrums with love of the music
I sing along with the songs
even if I don't know all the artists
the beat is catchy and fast
thrumming through me

but I don't know how to dance to fast songs
so I stand on the sidelines
nodding to the rhythm

and let girls like
Surly Girl and Sour Pout and Smirk Sister
show off in the center of eyes.

Somehow they've been practicing.
I'm not sure how.
Maybe they have moms or sisters or cousins
who show them.

I stand against the wall watching
Surly Girl freak Mean Boy
to Salt-N-Pepa's "Push it"
looking like it's her anthem
like she has always known how to move.

I wish I could finally feel comfortable
in my own skin
enough to dance
and let the music move my body
like I can in the privacy of the trailer

and FOR ONCE
not care what everyone else
is thinking.

A Note from your Author:

Yep, two chapters about practicing dancing
and then not putting my practice into practice
at the actual dance.

What I wish I'd known:

People judge you whether you are on the dance floor or not.
You may as well get out there
and shake your stuff with the rest of them.

Life's short.

Dance whenever

wherever

you can.

MOTHER'S DAY

Mother's Day comes before I'm ready
and I forget to make anything for either of my moms.

But Bronja has plenty: two cards, some gifts for both of them
and I realize how empty my hands are.

After brunch Sharon pulls me into the house.
"Your mom is hurt that you didn't do anything for her
for Mother's Day. She feels really unappreciated."

My heart hollows out my body as it drops.
I feel so full of awful I don't know what to do with myself.

I realize that it may be partly
because of the secret that is now unsecret
that I haven't gotten them anything
haven't done something for Mother's Day
for the first time in ever.

I am still carrying the scars from that wildfire day
even though I won't talk to them about it
like I am trying to punish them for it a little.

I make myself sick.

I go to the back room to find Mom
shoulders hunched from hurt.
I put my arms around her and tears are everywhere
tangled with apologies and appreciations
I didn't bother to put on paper.

I think about Bronja, the not-Real Daughter who remembered

while I, Real Daughter, am all
thoughtlessness and *I'm sorries*,
shame and regret.

TRYING TO OWN IT

One gray day, I walk home with Iris
dynamic-funny-cute-pretty-perfectly-paired-brand-name-outfits-
Iris,
and it is a milestone.

This is a girl who didn't seem to like me all year
who I always secretly wanted to be friends with
but who always seemed too
Everything.

But here we are
on a moody gray spring-almost-summer day
the close clouds seem
appropriately heavy
and our conversation is deep, real
weighted like those clouds:

her difficult father who lives in Mexico
her big crush on a boy named Dave
her insecurity about her body
her also being an only child

and it is

Then

when I decide to tell her about my mom
even though of course she probably has heard.
But it is my first purposeful
intended, not-a-kid-anymore
un-forced telling:

"My mom's gay.
She's been with her partner for six years.
Sharon's like my other mom."

"Wow. What's that like?"

Iris wants to know what it's like. What is it like?

I tell her:
"Sometimes it's cool, because
Sharon is really fun and less overprotective.
And she's way different than my dad
he's so difficult, kinda like yours."

She asks, and I tell
and in the telling
I am creating something new.

Un-Secreting myself
I watch as
some part of the Shame shakes away.

This is my story, and she wants to hear it.

As I talk this green growing hope
rises higher from the scorched earth
and I am starting to consider what it is like
this two-gay-moms thing
when it's not just a secret I am keeping.

She tells me her mom's best friend is a gay guy
and a door opens between us.

When we reach my street rain drops have started to fall
and we stand longer, as the wet circles pattern the pavement
quench this thirsty ground.

I feel closer
and more real
with someone
than I have in a long time.

BIRTHDAY ANTICIPATION

My twelfth birthday
the last before I become a real teenager
is on Sunday, and is celebrated
just with my family.

My birthday party will be dinner the Saturday before
with a handful of good friends.

I wonder what my mom and Sharon
have gotten me
even though I don't deserve anything
the way I forgot Mother's Day
and hastily made belated cards to make up for it.

I wonder what Bronja has gotten me
even though I don't deserve anything
the way I've been giving her the cold shoulder.

Sometimes all I want is a room of my own
where I can shut the door and cry to myself.

I cannot wait for school to be out
and it'll only be a couple of weeks now.

We have my birthday
and Bronja's prom
and then summer will be here
and Bronja will be leaving
and we will move into our newly remodeled house
that has somehow grown, day by day
into a thing we will finally live in.

Best of all:
soon I will be free from
Middle School Hell
for two whole months.

BIRTHDAY DAY

I open my eyes to the view
from my too-tight bunk
of our everything-tiny trailer.

I take in the sights blurry and fuzzy with my bad eyes
and then remember:

It's my birthday.

My actual, real birthday. I am 12.
I feel flutters of excitement
and small anchors of dread.

What if they don't remember?
What if no one gets me anything?
I sort of deserve that.

I rub my eyes and
look down to Bronja's bed
where there is no Bronja.

Hmm.

Where is she?
I try to remember hearing the creak-slam
of the trailer door
but I can't tell if it's only in my imagination
after hearing that same creak-slam
so many times a day over the last three months.

And then the door creak-squeaks open
and there is my mom
with a tray of biscuits fresh from the oven
in our new kitchen that the workmen
finished just last week.

I smell their wheaty-warm goodness
as it fills our trailer
and there, in her hand
is the little bowl of dough covered in a paper towel
the small crescents she saves for me after
she is done cutting the biscuit rounds.

"Happy Birthday to you…"
She sings, with Sharon and Bronja's voices filling in with her.

I slide down from the bunk
throw a robe over my pj's and smile at my family
their loving eyes all looking at me
as they sing me my 12th birthday wishes.

Sharon holds the bowl of eggs
Bronja has the hash browns and fresh-squeezed OJ.

I realize: they must have all gotten up
sometime in the earliest hours
to get it ready for me this morning
in our house kitchen that's finally functioning.

My eyes tear up a little
thinking of how they planned this just for me:
the moody almost-teen who has been
a huge pain to live with for months now.

They still love me, the sullen sulking girl
even though I'm awful so much of the time.

We scoot into our too-small folding dining room table
and gather around the plates.
We are four women
nestled in close to each another
feasting on delicious food made for me

and all my rainbowed complexity.

PROM PICTURES

Bronja is really doing it.
She's going to prom with her
girl   friend
Belinda.

Bronja is decked in a tux with tails
her hair slicked back, kinda in drag.
Belinda's in a royal blue notice-me ball gown
curvy like a mermaid from Caribbean seas.

They come to our place before heading to prom
and take funny photos in the back yard
sitting on our old toilet
that's living on the grass for the moment.

Belinda sits on Bronja's lap
in the shade of our new two-story home
that looms high and wide, like something enormous
parked on top of where our old home used to be.

They take serious photos
and giggly photos
and I don't sense romantic feeling between them
just possibility and pretending.

I wonder if you are braver in high school.
How is it that you start to be more confident
more secure in "who you are."

How will I stop worrying about what people think?
Will I ever?

Is that even possible for me:
the only child
the constant worrier
the bad-skinned girl

always longing for Pretty?

How will I ever have the courage to stand up
for what I know is right?
To stand up for myself?

What will I say about my mom and Sharon
when I am older, hopefully wiser
less intent on pleasing others?

And who will I take prom pictures with?

LAST GASPS OF SIXTH GRADE

I'm not any better at sports
but PE has become
one of my favorite times of day.

I've started to walk the field on run days with Reina.

She is a little shorter than me
way curvier, green eyes, a nose she can't stand
zits that aren't as bad as mine, but that she groans about
which makes me feel she gets my agony.

What is it about skin?

Reina is funny
and bold and smart-mouthed
maybe like Sharon was
when she was our age.

She is fearless with teachers, sometimes rude
which makes me both deeply cringe
and feel awful for the teacher-target
and secretly thrill that I am friends with such a rebel.

She is smart
but questions authority in a way
I never do.

I love hanging out with her
and for some reason
I don't understand
she loves hanging with me.
We lap the big field
and tell secrets.

It's a bit like how I felt on that walk home with Iris
when a door opened with someone new

but with Reina, it seems
like she actually has time for me
seeks me out
whereas Iris is so friend-full.

One of the first laps
I tell her about my mom and Sharon
~though of course she may already know~
which Reina thinks is so cool.

I can't believe it.
Someone my age actually sees this
two-moms lesbian thing
as a *good* thing?

With such a reception the stories pour out:

My eggshell weekends with my scary dad.
Her daily battles with her angry dad.
My mom and Sharon and
the current state of our demolished, fractured home.
Reina's memories of their exhausting remodel.
Reina's annoying little sister who she loves and hates.
Bronja's temporary sisterhood which I love and hate.

We talk and talk
palm notes at passing period
talk about other girls
and pass judgment on the nastiest ones:
the Surly Girls and the Sour Pouts.

We talk about boys we have crushes on
we talk about what we might do
or would never do
with boys we have crushes on.

Reina is sensitive and insecure
but also bold and outrageous.

She is the Best Friend I have been hoping for.

Our friendship unfolds with some of the
same feelings I imagine dating does:
the initial noticing
the rush of laughter
connection and attention.

The talking for hours on the phone
the getting to know each other's secrets
the tentative trust
the budding loyalty
the promises and proclamations:

I'll never tell anyone.
It's just between us.
You are my Best Friend.

I wonder if this is a kind of practice for dating
if somehow friends prep each other
for romantic relationships this way.

All I know is
I'm so glad that I've been chosen
that someone accepts me
all of me
for who I am.

And I think it is getting me closer to

One Day

being able do that for myself.

MAYBE SECRETS ARE SEEDS

small, portable pods
of vital material
precious cargo
things we need to survive

our truths, our core, our light

how this small seed sparked to life
in middle school wildfire
sprouted, rooted, widened

and—like seeds, the roots
connected me to others
strengthened bonds
or tested them

maybe gave others a chance
to grapple with buried things too

their own vital truths
look at themselves anew

maybe, in the flame of rumor
this seed-secret deepened shared roots

gave a small morsel of representation~
Gay folks can be good parents too!

maybe secrets are seeds
and when shared

which is to say
planted

between people
given good earth and loving light

showered maybe with a few tears
given a little space to shine

they root into webs of connection
deep bonds, intertwined and reaching
toward the seed-truths of others

how a secret
when shared
allows others
to share too

allows others
to speak out
or stand up
or stand with

how
when they find the light
seeds and secrets
can blossom into
something beautiful

which is to say

True.

After Ode

QUONSET HUT OF LOVE

was what my Mamas called each other
in the early years

Quonset huts:
prefabricated temporary military structures
170 thousand or so built in World War II

turned song of sweetness between them
those two women who turned to women
before women loving women turned chic

Quonset huts: corrugated galvanized half-domes
unassuming from the Quonset outset
requiring no skilled labor to assemble

shippable anywhere: later the surplus
found new homes in countless places

semi-circular rust resistant flexible interior spaces
something that could pop up and protect
as needed, wherever

I never knew where they got this term of endearment from
never asked in the depths of childhood's thrum

what made these two women
one Brooklyn-born, one Texas-torn
sing songs of corrugated galvanized half-domes

my Mamas~my Maps~my Refuge~my Home

all bare-boned basic
rust resistant, flexible, spacious

all peace and love
and war-zone ready.

Acknowledgments

The irony of taking 12 years to publish a book about secrets is a lovely reminder of the ongoing work of self-acceptance.

I started this book in 2012 as I wrote alongside my middle school students during National Novel Writing Month. It began as a novel, then shifted to memoir with inspiration from the LGBTQIA+ rights movement that points us all toward greater inclusivity and love.

This book is an ode to sisterhood seeded in middle school—my girls Alli, Chris, Jasmin, Jen, Kat, and Virg. Across all the years and all the miles, our friendship has buoyed and blessed me. You inspire me and keep me laughing at all the ways we are still growing up and finding ourselves. For an only child, I have the most amazing pack of sisters.

Much love to Bronja Glaser for joining our rainbow family during that pivotal time and helping tween me broaden my narrow perspective.

Another chosen sister emerged in my college years and helped this book join the world. Tamar, we met as horses in *Equus*, and later, saw each other through Brown in our turbulent late adolescence. Thank you for reading this book and offering vital insights and edits.

When I began my career in education in 2001, I returned to the messy magic of middle school. I was supported in this worthy work by my teaching brothers: Bill, Erich, Kane, Larry, and Mike. Thank you for guiding and inspiring me through middle school, round two.

Later, my educator family grew when I finally headed off to teach high school. So much love to the Queens who got me through pando-teaching with love and laughter: Carolyn, Chris, Jennie, Kirsten, Sophie and Trasey. Gratitude to Maxine and Rachel for reading this work and celebrating middle school Haze, and to Julia whose excitement buoyed me in the doldrums. Cheers to the ELA Department, STEMM crew, and my VHS family who keep me loving my day job with hugs, high fives, and *how you holding ups*? What a tremendous community—I'll dance the line with you anytime.

I am so grateful for the family of friends I've gathered later in life: Raf (who joined the family further when he married Kat!), Court and Miranda, Max and Paige, Jaz's Dave, Brian and Katie, Megan and

Andrew, Erick and Megan. Cheers to the Family Dinner Crew I survived my twenties with. Love to my NICU sister Nkechi and the ways we created family when we needed it most. Love to the friends my children have brought through their friendships: Sierra and Rob, Jenn and Jon, Mary-Claire and John, Toby and Guri, Jessica and César.

To the cover crew! What a saga…Huge gratitude to AlyssaBeth Archambault for her cover notes, artistic eye, and font-genius. Thanks to Tyler Fister for cover consultation and Mr. Serna for rallying artistic support. Thanks to Elizabeth Fernandez for designing one draft of the cover and patiently incorporating my many notes and requests. Thanks to Steve Lewis for generously giving time and expertise to help me revise the cover on one of the many passes. Boundless gratitude to my former roommate Eileen who made a career in teaching an art form AND swooped in to help finalize the cover into a glorious galaxy.

I have been blessed by great teachers, wise guides through all the wildernesses: Mrs. McDowell (Kinder), Ms. Stangl (2nd), Ms. Feuerstein, Ms. Lawson, and Ms. Reed (middle school), Ms. Karr and Ms. Wong-Nichols (high school), and Mrs. Mains, Natalie White, Kate Lipkis, and Kate Kausch as I became a teacher myself—so many brilliant women opened my heart to stories and writing, literature and listening. Gratitude to the Ojai Foundation and the art of Council. Here's to circling up and sharing stories to connect with our truest selves.

Awe and delight for all my students who teach me so much, give me hope for our world, and ground me in the wonder of words and writing. You make teaching the best job there is. Love to Mary for supporting our family during pando, helping us navigate that wild time.

So much gratitude to the Get Lit/Words Ignite community, who turned me into a slam poetry coach. The literary liberation and student nurturing Get Lit fosters is second to none. Eternal love to Diane, Laurie, Kelly, Brian, Raul, Mason, Aman, Austin, the whole Get Lit galaxy of stars. You make spring semester SHINE.

Love to VHS Gondo slam poets, Shara, Danielle, Jayden, Aires, Drew, Ollie, Andrew, Ernesto, Emily, Mya, Virginia, Ayesyz, Kenza, Jenna, Libby, Dibora, Jason, Summer, Camila, Elize, Amy, Jonathan, Jaylen, Sam, Zara, Aarna, Prianna, and co-coach, Sam Cline. It took nine years to take first, but you all are champions of all that is good and true and beautiful.

In my early teaching years, the Language Arts Cadre, UCLA Writing Project, and Jane Hancock and Faye Peitzman helped me claim the title of writer. My UCLAWP writing group was vital kinship: Carrie Usui Johnson, Reynaldo Macias, Kendra Nichols Wallace, and Sarah Orgill, cheers to laughing, listening, and swapping pages. Thanks to Erin Powers and Dan Buccieri for inspiration and integrity in the work.

I was surrounded by brilliant mentors in my MFA program at Antioch University Los Angeles, people who assured me my stories matter: Bernadette Murphy, Sharman Apt Russell, Leonard Chang, Terry Wolverton, and Emily Rapp Black. Cheers to Jenny Factor and Wendy C. Ortiz for early conversations about our rainbow families.

Thanks to our Antioch Alum crew of Haunted Weekend Orioles for warm feedback on early drafts of this book: Jane O'Keefe, Lisa McCool-Grime, Seth Fischer, Josh Indar, Neal Bonser, and Scott Miller.

I continue to collect mentors in the literary luminaries I share this unique time on earth with. Writer-Boss Roxane Gay, Delight Deliverer Ross Gay, Sheer Genius Jesmyn Ward, Web-Weaver Ruth Ozeki, Radiant Historian Rebecca Solnit, Luminous Ada Limon, Story-Mapper Alexander Chee. The ones who legacy on: Toni Morrison, Maya Angelou, Lucille Clifton, Gwendolyn Brooks. Mary Oliver, one day we'll walk the woods together. These writers and more have helped me live new lives through their words.

In my post-MFA life, the visionary organization Women Who Submit has been an extraordinary reconnect to the safety and strength of an inclusive, women-centered, queer-celebrating community. Special shout-outs to the pando Saturday morning check-ins group, including Ryane Granados, Tisha Marie Reichle-Aguilera, Toni Ann Johnson, Xochitl-Julisa Bermejo: you all help me dream into a brighter world, and you helped make this book join the world. Huge gratitude to Flint for an early, enthusiastic read and supportive coaching on the cover.

Thank you to the generous community-builder Cody Sisco and the Made in L.A. team. I'm grateful for your support of my L.A. writing.

Much love to Denise Kiernan for early, ongoing support of this story. Thanks to my first agent, Hannah Gordon Brown: while we didn't sell it back in 2015, we did make it stronger. Thanks to Rita Rosenkranz who offered wisdom and guidance. Gratitude to agents Rebecca Eskildsen and Stephen Barr who read and gave notes. Big thanks to Lindsey and Matt Barr for cheering me on—your words helped hush the doubt.

Thank you to *For Women Who Roar* for first publishing versions of "Quonset Hut of Love," "Pride Before the Fall," and "The Talk."

Wellstone Center in the Redwoods gives my writing partner Noriko and me needed space for our writing lives. So much love to Steve and Sarah and Sally and the girls for creating this favorite writing refuge.

Thanks to Dorland Mountain Arts retreat and the staff, especially Janice, for making a place for writers to focus on their creative lives. You brought me new and renewed writing family in Danny Getzoff, Kim Steutermann Rogers, Pam Woolway, and Jen Wyrauch Edson, all of whom cheered me on to chart a new path for this book.

Love and light to my dad, Roy, and my gone-too-soon stepmom, Patti. Gratitude for the step-siblings I was granted later in life: Joel and Freddy, Ruth and Jack, Nate and Elyse and Rick. Love to my LA cousins Casey, Matt and Robin for helping me gain a sense of siblinghood.

Love to my Texas family, Mike and Jason, Brianna and Max, and dear Betsy. Love to the family Sharon gave me: Samantha and Adam, Kenny and Zina, the cousins and the family of friends: Renee and Donna.

Much love to the family I was so lucky to marry into: my dear in-laws Sheila and Charles, dearly departed in-laws Barry and Peg. Love to brothers Mike and Adam and Chaz, Cara and the cousins—thank you for welcoming this L.A. girl to the family.

Love to the Maine family: Kimmie Kat and Joey, Troy and Dawn; the Indy crew of Aunt Wendy, Sara and Zach, and the young ones; the Rackliffs and Claytons: here's to all island projects and happy hours, long walks and bog-hole plunges, sunset cheers and twilight wiffle ball. You all make that place we share so very special. Love to the Seattle and Austin Wilkersons, and all German Withams who have recently taken up residence in our hearts. Our family is a tremendous web.

This work celebrates my moms and the home they made for me, one that included a strong web of wonderful women. Huge love to Moe and Jo, Star and Dalia, Karen and Karen and Barbara. You fill our home with laughter and warmth, offering spacious, generous views of loving and living. Love to Renate and Lloyd for being an early second family.

My eternal gratitude lives on for Sharon, my bonus mom, my calm mom, my mom gone too soon. Every day I feel her legacy. When I'm stretching myself thin, burning the candle at both ends, I can still hear her voice, saying: "Relax, Haze. Take it easy. It's going to be alright."

To my dear mama Judie: you continue to support me and our family every day with such generosity, humor, and love. You patiently listen and marvel at the non-stop whirlwind of our blessedly full lives. I know it all must be exhausting at times, but you continue to be my greatest refuge, my truest home. I love you so.

My boys G and C are the most delightful humans I have had the honor of watching join this world, awakening to all its wonder and complexity. I am awestruck by you both and can't wait to see the paths you chart for yourselves, the stories you will write. May you treasure your siblinghood and strive toward peacemaking over battle-planning.

To my writing partner Noriko Nakada, one of the great friendships of my life. Thank you for patiently reading drafts and listening to revisions, across so many early writing mornings, writing dates, and writing retreats. You stuck with me through the long process of shaping the work, cheered me on when the doubts bullied in, and reminded me with every pass that I could defy the gatekeepers altogether. I am so grateful to you for the home ~~Strikethrough~~ Press gave this book.

For Drake, my beloved, the man who first suggested I focus tightly on that pivotal day and take the reader through the many awkward, transformative moments, period by period. Thank you for patiently reading and listening to the work over these dozen years. Your editorial and comedic instincts are the finest I know. Your unwavering support kept me returning to the page to refine it again and again. Thank you for all the space you help me carve out for my creative life, and all the joy and laughter you've brought to our shared world. You will always be my book champion.

And finally, to You, Dear Reader. Thank you for reading. It is a long-awaited sweetness, knowing you are out there somewhere, revisiting the wilderness of middle school, mapping your own way through the woods. Here's to honoring our secrets and owning our truth.

Praise for **THE TRUTH ABOUT SECRETS**

Deft, lyrical and richly rendered, Hazel Kight Witham transports us into "the galaxy of secrets swirling inside" her sixth-grade self—including the secret ticking like a shame bomb and threatening to blow up her life.
~**Flint, author of** *Blood*

Hazel Kight Witham's book is a love poem to mothers, chosen family, and forgotten heroes. As a child of the 80s, her story recalls a bright bubbly era that's insides crowded with doubt, hate, and alienation. Now as the nationalist call for conformity once again bellows loud and scary, Kight Witham's story is a beacon to all us lonely truth tellers. She reminds us that speaking the truth for the sake of love can never be wrong.
~**Xochitl Julisa Bermejo, author of** *Posada: Offerings of Witness and Refuge* **and** *Incantation: Love Poems for Battle Sites*

Hazel Kight Witham offers beautiful and often painful truths about surviving middle school in a time before technology mitigated relationships. She captures the rhythm of pre-adolescent conversations and thoughts, the halted awkward movement of pubescent bodies. She frames her life with two moms among the realities of time and place, giving readers a way to find connection and the opportunity to recall their own unique experiences. Battling the inner turmoil that secrets create, young Hazel scurries in and out of her own mind, struggles to find herself in the crowd of people she thinks will not accept her or understand her family dynamics.

We watch her growth and witness the influences on her transformation. Along this adolescent journey, Hazel interjects her adult wisdom in "A Note from Your Author" to provide young readers a bit of necessary hindsight. She offers adult readers advice too: "You just might remember how hard it is to be a kid sometimes."
~**Tisha Marie Reichle-Aguilera, author of** *Breaking Pattern*

In the tradition of *The Poet X*, Hazel Kight Witham's memoir-in-verse captures the anxiety and dreams of a middle school girl in the 1980's with a serious crush and a secret — her mom is a lesbian. The narrative moves between poetry and prose, and between a fateful day at school and the author's reflections where she inserts moral questions and an LGBTQ+ 101 primer in a teacherly way. The book builds through these vignettes of mixed nostalgia and horror into a revelation in which courage beats shame. Read it with a young person, or with your inner young person, when you're feeling nostalgic for a future when LGBTQ+ people and their families can love without fear.
~Brian Sonia-Wallace, 4th West Hollywood City Poet Laureate, author of *The Poetry of Strangers: What I Learned Traveling America with a Typewriter*

This is a great work of storytelling that captures you from the jump like a smash hit rap hook or a Taylor Swift song mired in based-on-a-true-story intrigue. The "truth" is rarely as crisp and lovely as Hazel Kight Witham's nostalgic memoir-in verse, which deftly uses dynamic free verse to tell a riveting coming of age narrative in short, quippy stanzas that create a sense of urgency that unravels like a mystery.

It's a fresh snapshot of the modern American century when society was grappling with challenges to a binary, puritanical "normalcy" that was probably never even real to begin with. At the same time, it feels like a piece of nostalgic whimsy, a throwback to Chaucer's Canterbury Tales told from the perspective of a teenage girl, a young woman, and a mom who all happen to be the same person—a person who starts like many great literary heroes as a "coward." Thankfully for us, Hazel grew up to be brave enough to write this book.
~Erick Galindo, creator of WILD and IDOLO podcasts

Hazel Kight Witham's *The Truth About Secrets* deftly captures the horrendous anxiety of being a middle-school girl rife with insecurities. It then raises the stakes exponentially with the added fear of being outed for having two moms. My heart broke for young Hazel, who loves her mothers and her unconventional family, but who struggles as most middle-schoolers do, with the stomach-dropping terror of not fitting in. Witham's skillful and authentic rendering of her adolescent interiority combined with her enormous wit and compassion made me laugh as hard as I cried reading this tour de force of a memoir in verse.

~Toni Ann Johnson, author of *Light Skin Gone to Waste*

Reading Recommendations

Here are a few books, many in verse, for young readers that inspire me and led in some way to the creation of this one.

The Poet X and *Clap When You Land* by Elizabeth Acevedo

The Crossover by Kwame Alexander

Speak and *SHOUT* by Laurie Halse Anderson

Posada: Offerings of Witness and Refuge by Xochitl-Julisa Bermejo

Out of the Dust by Karen Hesse

Totally Joe by James Howe

Through Eyes Like Mine, Overdue Apologies, and *I Tried*: a memoir trilogy by Noriko Nakada

Queer, There, and Everywhere: 23 People Who Changed the World by Sarah Prager

Breaking Pattern by Tisha Marie Reichle-Aguilera

Long Way Down by Jason Reynolds

Stop Pretending: What Happened When my Big Sister Went Crazy (the first book-in-verse I ever read!) and *What my Mother Doesn't Know* by Sonya Sones

Brown Girl Dreaming by Jacqueline Woodson

About the Author

Hazel Kight Witham is a mother, educator, writer, and slam poetry coach who grew up in Los Angeles and still calls it home. She earned a B.A. from Brown University and an M.F.A. in Creative Writing from Antioch University Los Angeles.

Hazel is a proud public school educator in LAUSD and was a 2020 finalist for California Teacher of the Year. Every November she shepherds students through National Novel Writing Month and each April finds her classes poeming daily for Poetry Writing Month. She leads workshops for educators on building a sustainable teaching practice.

Hazel's writing explores issues of wellness, healing, social justice and peace-making and can be found in literary journals including *The Sun*, *Bellevue Literary Review*, *Mutha Magazine*, *High County News*, and *Cultural Weekly*. She is committed to a world where creativity and kindness overpower the screens and machines. *The Truth About Secrets* is her first book.

Made in the USA
Las Vegas, NV
27 July 2024